12 Habits of
Successfully Booked Up
Wedding Suppliers

Title ID: 6027423

ISBN-13: 978-1523717590

ISBN-10:1523717599

DEDICATION

'The 12 Habits' is dedicated to:

My mother, Mabel Lewis, for the struggle you went through raising my four siblings and I, practically single handedly on the notorious Chalkhill Council Estate in Wembley. Thank you for the values you taught me. You are an inspiration mum, and I love and respect you endlessly.

To my beautiful partner Julie Morrow, thank you for the belief you hold in me, the endless love you give and the support I can always depend on. Writing this book would be much less fun without you in my life. I will always be in love and thankful and honoured that you have chosen to share your incredible life with me.

My children, Portia, Ella, Brandon and Jordan, I love you all. This book is to remind you of something my favourite primary school teacher Leslie Francis wrote in a dictionary she gave me when I was just 11 years old: "Always have confidence in yourself."

Abbey Orebanwo – for the friendship, wisdom, and life lessons you continue to teach me in abundance. You are more than a brother to me.

To my family who supported me during the high and low points in my life; Everton, Joetta, Avis, Richard, Ian, Tracey and Sheena, thank you for helping me discover the light at the end of the tunnel, your words of encouragement and support have helped me more than you know.

To Bryan Bertram, thanks for the support you gave my mum and family.

The wedding creatives from The Ultimate Wedding Entertainment mastermind group who've inspired and helped me: Alan Marshall, Anthony Winyard, Barney Grossman, Brian Mole, Euan Bass, Gary Evans, Harry Kilb, Iain Baker, Mark Walsh, Paul Forsyth, Paul Taylor, and Steve Mitchell. By sharing your collective wisdom and the synergistic ideas that were born out of our sessions, I was able to take giant steps. It is because of you that my career took off, and for that I'll be forever thankful and humbled to each of you for the individual parts you have played in my success.

Hollie Kamel, thank you for your support and friendship, you have always been there for me and I will never forget that. You mean a lot to me.

Mark and Rebecca Ferrell, you set me on the path to delivering weddings at the next level through the Master of Ceremonies speaking skills you taught me. Never stop doing what you do because your creativity brings a deeper emotion to weddings... globally.

Moe Nawaz, author, speaker and strategic advisor to FTSE 100 companies, thank you for giving me a free scholarship within your Mastermind group at The Ritz London which contributed to the re-focusing of my business, including finishing this book. The lessons you taught me fast-tracked my progress. To each of Moe's Mastermind group members who've challenged, pushed and shared wisdom with me, I thank you too.

Some of the people who I do not personally know but have inspired and helped me through a combination of live experiences, books, audio MP3's or online modems include: Adam Witty, Amy Porterfield, Anthony Robbins, Brian Tracy, Bernadette Doyle, Brendon Burchard, Chris Cardell, Dale Carniege, Dan Kennedy, Eban Pagan, Grant Cardone, John C. Maxwell, Michael E. Gerber, Napoleon Hill, Pat Flynn, Robert T. Kiyosaki, Seth Godin, Sir Richard Branson and Stephen R Covey.

For the teachings that follow I give credit to all the above influencers and thought leaders for helping me shape the ideas I now present to you through these writings.

Finally, I give thanks to God, my creator through whom all things are possible.

CONTENTS

FOREWORDS

By Damian Bailey

The Wedding Industry Awards (TWIA)

Founder and Managing Director

Terry's excellent reputation within the wedding industry in the UK is second to none. The 12 Habits is accessible, packed with ideas and is of real value to anyone who really wants to ensure that their business stands out from the crowd.

Whether you are just starting out and want to hit the ground running or have been running your wedding business for a while and want to rise to the next level, this is your chance to listen to and learn from someone who has created and maintained an incredibly successful wedding business.

The wedding industry is a highly competitive marketplace worth an estimated £10 billion each year (source: www.hitched-wife.org). The insights disclosed in this book will give you a positive advantage in getting your share. Invaluable.

By Alison Hargreaves

Guides for Brides

Director

Terry takes widely accepted best business practices and applies them to the wedding industry, adding his own experience and anecdotes along the way. Practical tips, sample scripts and checklists ensure that by the time you finish the book you have a clear understanding of where you want your business to go and how to get it there.

To find out more about Damian and Alison please see Acknowledgements.

INTRODUCTION

Around 12 years ago I announced to a close friend, *"I'm reading a book on how to build a successful business!"* He impulsively asked *"Terry, does the author have a successful business?..."*

His curve ball stopped me dead in my tracks and the more I thought about his simple question, the clearer the wisdom of his short lesson became. He went on to say, "Terry before you take advice from anyone in life, first ensure they have achieved what it is they are advising you to do, or you may not get the results you are hoping for."

My friends name is Abbey Orebanwo, and I have never forgotten his simple schooling, and it's the first lesson I am passing onto you.

MY STORY

In 2010 I was being underpaid by a wedding venue I was given regular work at.

I was conditioned into believing the low pay offered was all I was worth and the fear of getting no work at all made me accept it. During peak times the venue gave me up to 4 weddings or events a week, and with 4 dependent children, the monthly pay albeit low helped with the bills. I was operating at the bottom of the barrel, and did little to crawl out of it.

It was very easy and very hard; easy because I just plodded along getting regular work at low pay, hard because I struggled to provide for myself and family. Is this something you can relate to? The truth was that by accepting the venue's offer of under paid work, I gave them permission to devalue me. I had created a bad habit of failure that was actually taking me in the opposite direction to where I wanted to go. Why? Well I knew of wedding creatives in my industry earning several times my rate but instead of discovering how they did it, I lazily waited for the call, text or email asking if I was available to take a booking at the meagre rates offered which I habitually accepted.

But it gets worse, my mindset was so distorted, when I marketed directly to brides and grooms I sold myself short thinking if I did not discount deep enough I would never win their business. I was on a roundabout to failure and I had no idea where the exit was that would lead to success.

Finally I took action.

By 2011, I experienced so much financial pain it caused problems at home.

Debt mounted. Our mortgage was in arrears. Letters in brown envelopes kept landing on the door mat. Change was forced upon me.

Albert Einstein is widely credited with the saying "The definition of insanity is doing the same thing over and over again, but expecting different results". But it was not until I stumbled upon the following words by John C. Maxwell, did I really understand the need for a new direction, he said:

"You'll never change your life, until you change something you do daily. The secret of your success is found in your daily routine."

"...found in your daily routine." – those final words repeated in my head like a stuck record, each time the wake-up call got louder until I could ignore it no more.

His truth pierced like a knife. How was I ever going to succeed if I clung onto bad habits? I needed to proactively take responsibility for my life and the lives of those who depended upon me. I had to change everything. I immersed myself in learning from the best teachers I had access to, via seminars, workshops, books, MP3's, online programs and networking groups. Over the next few years I learnt to create a new set of empowering beliefs about who I could become and what I could achieve. I looked up at the summit and promised myself – I'd get there.

Why listen to me?

I have already stood in the middle of your shoes.

I know what it is like because I once struggled to get listed at luxury wedding venue's, failed with magazine adverts, had a website that was placed so low on Google I was practically invisible. I was often price shopped by venue's and brides wanting my services and attracted nowhere near enough bookings to avoid the famine and feast cycle. I realised that to get what successful wedding creatives had, I had to do what successful wedding creatives did. That meant becoming a gatherer of wisdom by tapping into the expertise of leaders both in and outside of the wedding industry. I took massive action, became seriously studious, applied the knowledge I learnt and restarted my wedding business with a new, really clear end goal in mind.

For me it started in the spring of 2011. I burnt the financial bridge connecting me to the underpaying venue by giving notice. I committed to change and that meant I had to burn any route that could take me backwards or make me change my mind. I told the venue I would see out my bookings until the year-end but wanted no more work thereafter other than literally a handful of events that I loved doing. In making that decision, I effectively stacked sticks of dynamite under the bridge providing a portion of my monthly income and pushed the detonator blowing it up. I felt amazing and relieved...for all of 10 minutes, then reality set in, I needed to replace, no massively increase that income. I believed I could do it, after all I'd given myself 7 months leeway until those venue bookings in my diary dried up. Surely it would be an easy task... but I failed myself again and again. It actually took me around 3 years to figure out how to position, package, promote and partner my brand so it became the natural choice to high paying brides. The thing is I never gave up. I had this deep burning inner self-belief that I could make it. I just had to keep trying and failing enough times because I knew eventually I would find a strategy that would work.

The very short version of how I did it

I created a premium wedding experience I knew only certain brides and groom's would love, it was never designed for everyone, just discerning couple's wanting the best. Alongside this I mastered the art of conveying value and articulating worth and this was the game changer.

By 2014 my fees were many times my 2010/11 rates yet bookings were at record levels, that's right I was actually winning more business than ever at up to 10x what I was previously paid. In fact at the time of writing I book around 70 weddings a year and now turn away a further 50 or so, due to excess demand. I had finally cracked the code on how to attract clients willing to pay my premium asking price, in abundance of my availability. Now I tell you this not to impress you but to express to you that it is possible to transform your wedding business through the strategies I teach, so you can succeed, live the life you deserve and simultaneously provide for those you love and care for.

Success leaves fingerprints; I've been blessed to have shaken the hands of many successful people. A lot of what I have learnt from others has rubbed off on the pages you are now turning. I wish I was able to hold a 'how to guide' like this during my formative years because I could have avoided so many mistakes, shortened my learning curve and found the fastest path to success.

I run one of the country's most successful solo operator wedding DJ businesses, but The 12 Habits is not about my industry at all, it's about the psychological, marketing and sales secrets that contributed to the phenomenal success I now enjoy on auto-pilot. Secrets that are applicable and transferrable across all sectors of the wedding industry including yours. I have advised venue owners, photographers, wedding planners, photo-booth operators, wedding singers, videographers, dj's and more, the industry does not matter, what does matter is your openness to change. What I teach are the essential business tools required to attract and book higher paying brides, and if you wonder why you are struggling to book your ideal clients and attract too many price shoppers, The 12 Habits will help you get really clear on the things you need to change.

By reading this book I already know some facts about you.

- *You have a burning desire, almost a need to succeed so you can better your life and the lives of those you love and care about.*

- *Average is too low a target for you, you plan to rise way above the ordinary wedding suppliers operating in your field of expertise. You need to succeed to fulfil your dreams.*

- *You may have struggled at school but you've never let that hold you back from thinking big with your wedding business.*

But there is a grain of sand in your oyster, a flaw that has so far stopped you from getting to the next level and it's your propensity to procrastinate. You know there are big things you have to get done to move the needle of your wedding business forward, but for some reason there is a block stopping you from taking action.

Today you've stepped up to the plate and through The 12 Habits you have the bat in your hand giving you the power to knock it out of the park but you've got to keep your eye on the ball and swing accurately. The strategies I will share with you have the power to ignite your wedding business, allowing it to really take-off and thrive in a way they have done for myself and the other wedding suppliers I advise.

The 12 Habits are your treasure map to wedding business success, but you have to follow through to maximise your opportunity. I'm about to share powerful secrets with you, but only you can make it happen.

I also believe it to be true of you that when it comes to your brides and grooms you fully show up for them and do everything in your power to ensure their wedding is the best day of their lives, but sometimes you don't always show up for yourself. I know that sometimes you put things off until tomorrow in favour of the path of least resistance. Procrastination is easy today but painful tomorrow. Promise yourself this time you will follow through to completion. Fulfil the challenges in this book with the dedication you give to your clients because it can change your life. It won't be easy, nothing worthwhile in life ever is but I can promise you this; you will eventually reap what you sow. Make this the moment you fully commit to yourself, make this the point at which procrastination no longer controls you.

Sporadically throughout 'The 12 Habits' you will see me lead a section with a **Red Flag**. Whenever you come across a red flag I really want you to pay attention and crush what ever it is that may be preventing you from owning the Habit in question, because it will be quintessential to you being able to thrive in your space.

Right now you have 2 choices: You can consume the contents of this book and either apply or deny them to your business. If Einstein and Maxwell's quotes resonate with you in the way they did for me, your decision has already been made for you...

THE FIRST HABIT

Amplify Your Message To A Very Specific Avatar Instead Of Trying To Sell To Everyone

You cannot successfully attract and book high paying brides to your wedding business without knowing what the profile of the perfect client looks like, so let's begin with that end in mind.

Who is your ideal client?

- *Do you try to sell to every bride and groom?*

- *Have you carved out a specialist niche within your market to elevate yourself above the other wedding suppliers crowding your industry?*

Let's look at two real life examples: *Primark* and *Harrods* are both well known successful departmental stores, targeting opposite ends of the market.

Harrods do not target *Primark* shoppers and *Primark* do not target *Harrods'* customers. Both brands have identified the profile of the shopper they want to sell to, and both have laser focused strategies to attract their targets with crystal clear marketing and sales messages.

Let me share an early mistake I made so you can side-step it. On starting out, I sent out a terribly confused marketing message that tried to capture any and everybody throwing a party. Through a lethal combination of naivety, inexperience and a desperation not wanting to miss any shoppers, I tried to capture both *'Primark'* and *'Harrods'* shoppers and every bride and groom in between. My marketing was scattered all over the place and unsurprisingly spectacularly unsuccessful. In fact that is actually being kind. My strategy was an epic failure!

I kidded myself I could sell to everyone! I did not realise the folly and impossibility of my misplaced goal. Unless I had millions to spend on advertising and a massive marketing team to implement the colossal task, how could I possibly sell to every bride? At the time of writing more than 230,000 couple's marry in the UK each year, and I wanted to physically book them all! Really?...

Furthermore, can you imagine the diverse wants, specialities, desires and aspirations of all those couples? How could I craft a single marketing message that would appeal to all of them? Exactly. I couldn't.

It would be like trying to get a letter to my cousin Roseanne in Barbados by flying over the island in a helicopter and throwing 20,000 copies of the letter I wrote from the chopper, hoping one would flutter down and land next to her on the beach, and that she would hopefully pick the copy up to read. Of course that personal letter would not resonate with anyone else who picked it up to read it because it was not personalised to interest them; the stranger would almost certainly discard it. It would be far better for me to print off one copy of my letter, put it in an envelope, write my cousin Rosanne's address on the outside then take it to the post office for special delivery and in so doing, can you see how I could practically guarantee my letter would actually reach her, my target audience?

In order for you to post your message directly to your ideal client you need to become crystal clear and very narrow on who your ideal client really is. Everybody is not your client.

Learn to think how your ideal client thinks. Ask yourself what are the problems connected to your industry that your bride and groom are worried about and want to avoid? What pleasure triggers are they drawn to? The way to succeed in the wedding industry space is to get inside your prospects head and join in the conversation they are already having with themselves, their intended and with the other people planning their wedding. Know and understand their deepest fears, wants and aspirations then design your wedding experience around the nucleus of their goals, presenting your wedding business as the perfect solution. Do this uniquely, passionately and with a magnetic appeal but most importantly, in a way that places you beyond competition. Get really detailed and narrow on who you want to speak to in all of your wedding marketing and sales messages. The clearer you can 'see' what prospects want, the more accurate you will be at designing and delivering your marketing message to them. So when your potential clients reads, hears or watches your marketing messages they will resonate directly with your flow and think you are speaking to their interests, needs and feelings in a similar way my cousin Rosanne's letter would speak directly to her.

Exercise: Identify your wedding avatar

The highest earning, most successful wedding professionals carefully research their audience and draw a really clear picture, or buyer persona of who they want as a client known as an avatar to help them stay focused. This was something I side-stepped for ages because it looked like a whole lot of work that I really did not want to do. At the time I was getting average results, but mentor after mentor kept saying the same thing to me, "Identify your avatar". "Get really clear on who your target audience is", and because I was hearing the same advice being repeated by so many leaders, I eventually paid attention and took action and got my avatar in my crosshairs - and the results to my bottom line were exponential. If you meet with internal resistance creating your avatar and procrastination creeps in, repel it and never let procrastination prevent you from achieving – crush it as soon a possible. You need to amplify your message to a specific person if you are to thrive in the wedding industry space.

To become really clear on who your ideal client is, describe your avatar in as much detail as possible. Let me help you get started...Now I know that the groom sometimes has a lead role in the wedding planning process but because in the vast majority of cases the responsibility falls on the bride, for the purpose of drilling down and getting as clear as possible on who you are targeting, I want you to choose a female, and because my avatar is also female, it is the reason why I refer to my ideal client as either 'a bride, her, or she' interchangeably throughout this book but they all mean the same thing, my avatar. OK, with that out of the way let's dig in and get started.

Reminisce about your best client, the wedding at which you had the most enjoyment serving at; the celebration where you delivered your best results, recall the bride who saw your value, purchased one of your top priced packages, and paid your worth without quibble. This is the perfect person you want to rediscover and serve again, and again and again; this is your avatar.

In the table on the next page, name your wedding avatar after the bride you have just thought of and complete her profile:

Tip: Focus on the detail as sharply as possible, this is not a 'one and done' exercise, it's something you want to obsess over and come back to regularly as you discover more and more about your perfect client. Add more descriptive cells each time you revisit your avatar profile.

Name	
Age	
Profession	
Approximate Income	
Was the wedding in a church or at the venue?	
What star rating did the venue have?	
Give a physical description of your avatar	
What's the biggest pain point your avatar wanted to avoid at her wedding	
What were the pleasure points that attracted her to you?	
Use 3 words to describe your avatar's idea of the perfect wedding	
Describe your avatar's ideal honeymoon destination	
What's your avatar's number 1 objection to buying your wedding experience	

Red Flag

Now you are much clearer as to who you want to attract and sell to, take an honest look at your on and offline marketing material. Does it speak directly to your avatar? When your ideal prospect consumes your content does it resonate within and compel her to take the next step? If it does, well done, let's move on; but if it does not, you must correct your message immediately, and this is not something you can afford to put on your back burner, it is quintessential you do it now. Never let procrastination steal your dream.

THE SECOND HABIT

Apply The 4 P's
Position, Package, Promote and Partner Your Business So You Only Attract Your Avatar

If you are currently getting more price shoppers than value shoppers, the miscommunication is most likely in your marketing message, your personal letter to your avatar. And because the greatest chance of someone forming an opinion of you is via your website, I would suggest your problem is based on how you display your wedding service through your shop window. The reason price shoppers are attracted to you at the moment is because you are appealing to them. And if you are appealing to price shoppers you are less likely to appeal to the discerning higher spender, the couple you really want to book; you see the way to attract and book your ideal client is found in the clarity of your message.

So how can you change all this?

I use to make the mistake of writing my own website. My poorly targeted message made me appear low to middle-end at best. There was no positive advantage communicated, no genuine unique selling points, it was simply a broad-brush website that appeared beige and blended in amongst the rest. I failed to significantly stand out. The result was I attracted the negotiating price shopper and literally unsold the high paying bride, who ironically was the very person I wanted to magnetise.

The turnaround came when I niched and got my avatar directly in my crosshairs. I binned my failing self-made website and had it professionally written by a designer to whom I gave a crystal clear brief to include being unique, passionate, risk-free and offering value above my avatar's desires. I wanted my site to irresistibly pre-sell. In addition to this I wanted my site to imply expense. Today my enquiries come in from value shoppers because of the way I 'talk' to them online. Yes from time to time price shoppers stray into my pond, and I know this because in their initial email enquiry they include something like 'I don't know if we can afford you but…' or 'we are on a budget…' another one of my favourites is "I'm sure you come at a high price…" and I delight in all those types of enquiries because they reaffirm my message talks to a specific person, and not the masses.

To attract couple's with higher budgets and avoid price shoppers you must appeal only to the former. Change your message, and you'll change your results. You want your avatar hunting you. But how do you do this?

It begins by offering a signature wedding experience that fulfils every one of your ideal client's needs pure and simple, and when you get this right in your communications, your product or service 'is' your marketing and will go a very long way to selling itself. In short the tighter you match your wedding experience to your clients inner most desires and dispel their fears, the more you will get booked. Start with your bride and groom's inner most needs at the centre of your solution then build your wedding experience around it. The key is to promote the desired outcome your avatar wants, and position your company as the best route for them to enjoy it.

Master the 4 P's and increase attraction to you avatar:

Positioning

Make it one of your career goals to go out there and literally own your niche. Boldly become the number 1 go-to person in your arena. Don't shy away from a desire to dominate your ground, make sure it's you who wins. Step up to the challenge and claim your place as the leader in your industry. Someone has to be number 1 right? I know of some wedding professionals who do not want to shine a light on all their talents for fear of what others in their line of business think. To this I remind you, you have to think like a bride, and a bride is thinking she wants the best, not second or third best, The Best. And you have to be what she wants if you really want her to book you. Let me put it another way, have you ever heard a bride say she wants an average or ordinary <state your profession>? As long as you are being truthful, never dumb down your talents and achievements for fear of what others might think; because if you don't promote the greatest aspects of your attraction, who will? Your marketing outlets are where you must shine the brightest, so promote your truth and shine.

Packaging

Is your on and offline presence talking directly to your avatar? Is it aligned in tandem with the dependable quality she is seeking? Is your higher paying wedding experience congruently reflected through all your branding, or is there a disconnect between how you market and the brilliance you actually deliver? If you have a poorly designed DIY website or brochure for example, you will be diluting your excellence and potentially unselling the people who find you. Extensive research shows your ideal client decides whether or not you are a good fit within 8 seconds of hitting your website. That's right you have just 8 seconds to magnetise her to your page. Is it possible that your avatar rapidly bounces simply because your first impressions falsely fail to impress? If you want to step up and win contracts from discerning brides willing to pay your higher than average prices, you have to step up your branding. Get everything professionally designed. If this passage speaks directly to you, it means it's time for you to do what winners do and that is to take immediate decisive action to fix the problem, and don't let procrastination steal your dream. Initiate a re-branding if you know your marketing material is currently doing you a huge disservice and does not accurately reflect your brand and the high service level you provide. You have to get all your ducks in a row, in the right order, that means if your skills have overtaken your on and offline promotions, you must realign them.

Promoting

The phrase 'best kept secret' is not something you want linked to your wedding experience at all, rather you need to amplify your message to be heard above the noise made by everyone else operating in your crowded wedding space. I've used the heading 'Promoting' purely for alliteration purposes though. A promotion is a one-off marketing effort run for a limited period of time, but it is not really the strategy I want you to adopt. Instead you need to engage in 'Campaigning'. A sustained series of long term marketing messages designed to engage and resonate with your avatar with intent to educate, influence and persuade her to take the next step towards booking you, and here's the takeaway, you never, ever stop campaigning.

Partnering

I go deeper on strategic partnering in Habit 10: 'Stop Dragging Buckets and Install Pipelines' but for now you should know that luxury wedding venue's, wedding suppliers and people who have experienced your creativity can spread your message far wider than you ever can, because there is a finite limit to the audience you are able to reach. The more partners you have promoting your wedding business the wider your circle of influence expands.

Once you have expertly mastered your craft and built a raving fan base for your wedding experience, others in your industry will notice you and will want to partner with you in ways that will help them and help you, thus creating a win-win cycle. Here's the thing, venues need suppliers to add spokes to their wedding wheel for it to spin smoothly. Let me give you an example: Gaynes Park is a premier wedding venue in Essex and it attracts couple's wanting a luxurious barn to stage their big day. Couple's hiring Gaynes Park are in sync with my avatar and I am both humbled and thrilled to be listed as one of Gaynes Park's expert wedding suppliers. At the time of this writing, Gaynes Park have more than 200 enquiries for next year's wedding season, and as a preferred wedding supplier, all these brides still looking for the services I offer will at some point be funnelled to me simply because I am on their preferred list. Of course brides have free will and don't have to book me, but the point is I am in an excellent position to win those I still have availability on, simply by being included on their list. The Juice is my campaigning is being done for me by this amazing award winning venue. That's potentially more than 200 targeted avatars poured into my marketing pipeline by someone else. It took me years of perseverance to get into this venue, it did not just land in my lap but my intent and determination to over-deliver every time I worked a wedding there paid off. Can you see how strategic partnering can lucratively help you attract and book high paying ideal clients to your wedding business? When you add the other forty or so venues I am also listed at from London to the edge of Essex, can you see how I am served up with an abundance of desirable avatars annually by other people? This does not even take into account the other pipelines I have provided by word of mouth, networking, Google, directories, wedding fairs, my website and social media. I want to reiterate that I do not tell you this to impress but rather to express to you what is possible when you get this right, and The 4 P's, combined with the talent to deliver a stellar service go a long way to setting you up to thrive.

This strategy aided through being excellent at what you do is the number one way to attract an abundance of hot enquiries at a very high level and I implore you to do whatever it takes to serve yourself up with a similar pumping pipeline of prospects. It is the best route to sustainable success in the wedding space.

Thinking back to my green years which began in 2008, I heard of wedding creatives that were regularly booking at the top end earning way more than I, but back then I had no idea how they were doing it; and this became the stuck record that was the soundtrack to my underperforming wedding business. It took me years to figure out what I was doing wrong and what I needed to do to change; and The 12 Habits will set out the steps you need to put in place to succeed. You are much more fortunate than I was at the start of my career, nobody was sharing the 'how to' strategies with as much transparency and detail as I will share with you through these pages. In fact, what I am disclosing through this writing are the exact steps I followed to attract and book an abundance of ideal brides.

In addition to The 4 P's, there are other known factors governing the buying decisions of couple's with higher wedding budgets and you must include them in your marketing and sales messages.

Be the best

Offering a personalised, exclusive, trustworthy experience with margin for you to over-deliver is a surefire way to magnetise your definition of the ideal bride to you.

High paying brides want exclusivity and they know that comes at a price. They do not want a cheap outcome nor a service that appeals to the masses. Exclusivity is key. In fact if your experience is too cheap the discerning bride will actually turn away from you. Did you know it is possible to 'un-sell yourself', by using the wrong trigger words when pitching? The following real-life story from a meeting I had with a couple planning their wedding exemplifies this: Making reference to a photographer they'd met at the same wedding fair they met me at, they recalled how he kept going on about how cheap his album range was and how much money they could save by using him and booking today.

They actually said to me *"Terry, price is not our main priority when choosing our photographer, what we want are stunning images of a high quality, he actually turned us off from even considering him with his bargain talk, we dreaded to think what the final pictures would look like!"* You see, discerning couples buy the belief of a transformative, brilliant and highly enjoyable outcome and and will always rank this desire above price.

By way of another example, a wine connoisseur would carefully select a wine flight to perfectly complement the food being served by the chef, and would never contemplate pouring plonk, despite being able to save a fortune, you see premium brides and grooms only want the best, low price is rarely at the top of their list when prioritising the factors that govern the buying decisions for their wedding. A fresher at university however may be delighted simply to be in possession of a bottle of vino to share with fellow students. It would be almost impossible to sell the same bottle of wine to the connoisseur and the fresher. Yet this is a classic error many wedding professionals make in trying to be all things to all brides. Failing to niche dilutes appeal, makes you more attractive to price shoppers and less attractive to the high-end.

Offer a one-off treat outside of your avatar's normal lifestyle to make them feel special

Another trait premium shoppers display is a desire to treat themselves on a one-off basis, such as their wedding. Beauty product giant L'Oreal know this so well, they built their *'Because I'm Worth It'* campaign around it.

Premium shoppers are not necessarily high income earners and from time to time include buyers who desire to experience something beyond their usual day to day lifestyle.

Project an aura of certainty if you want to magnetise premium couples

Better quality is usually associated with a higher price point. Ross Harvey is a friend of mine whom in the past has been awarded Best Wedding Photographer in the World by Junebug. As of this writing, his lowest priced package is 3 times that of the top package of many other wedding photographers I know, and his work as you can imagine is breathtaking, just Google him, you'll see exactly what I mean. Despite price, Ross is in very high demand both in the UK and abroad, his premium prices are not a deterrent to his avatar. The overriding force behind a discerning couple selecting Ross as their wedding photographer is the next level pleasure they will gain through his amazing work and the avoidance of disappointment associated with bad wedding photography.

Offer exclusivity, something special to talk about

Before embarking on my career as a wedding DJ, I worked for the FTSE 100 company Legal & General Investment Management, specialising in corporate investments. An Account Manager whom I worked with announced his engagement and chose the Middle Temple situated in London's legal quarter as his wedding venue. I discovered it was built in the 1500's and survived the Great Fire of London and both World War I and II.

I also found out that the first performance of Shakespeare's Twelfth Night was staged there in 1602, and that the bench in The Hall was thought to have been a gift from Elizabeth I.

What's more, the engagement scene from Bridget Jones - The Edge of Reason was filmed outside the Queens Room and that His Royal Highness, Prince William of Wales was called to the Bench in The Hall on 6 July 2009.

Do you think by staging his wedding in The Middle Temple my colleague and his then fiancé were giving their friends and family something exclusive and special to talk about in the run-up to their wedding? Do you think the Middle Temple is able to charge premium rates solely based on their unique selling points? Points no other venue globally could copy?

Do not underestimate the power of exclusivity, it lies at the root of being able to charge a premium for your wedding business. Your name, brand, reputation and USPs dictate your earning power.

To attract and book higher paying brides I urge you to create powerful USPs. In fact in the passage below I explain why it is essential you do so.

The advantage of a positive advantage

Your positive advantage should be built not on one, but several desirable, unique selling points over and above those of your competitors. Having just one USP is old school and will not cut it in today's competitive wedding space. Your genuine USPs will translate into your positive advantage. They will be accolades you will have to work very hard at to attain. Goals you will achieve that you are passionate about, and challenges you'll hurdle that your competitors will fall short at, effectively locking them out. Once acquired, stack your magnetic, synergistic and highly desirable USPs next to one another, then tip them over one by one in all your on and offline marketing promotions and campaigns and watch how they create a domino effect resulting in a steady stream of high paying bookings from couple's who will be drawn to you. This advantageous way to promote relies heavily on you being not good, but excellent at what you do, in effect, matching the desires of your avatar in ways your competitors find almost impossible to replicate, positioning you at the top in the eyes of your bride and groom. This is the most effective way of creating barriers to entry to your field of expertise and in doing so you'll isolate yourself in a niche market where there is no competition for what only you can do, making it impossible for couple's to compare you on price because you have no other equal. This will allow you the comfort of operating in an arena where you become the natural choice. By way of example, technology giant Apple are the epitome of a company which has mastered the principle of the positive advantage. Many companies sell similar products, yet Apple dominates the market...globally. You must avoid being just another runner on the field of play, I see you as an over achiever and for you it's not the competing that counts it's the winning. What can you do to move the needle towards being the 'Apple' of your wedding industry, dominating your sector? Do not shrink back from this tough challenge if you really want to thrive.

A word of warning, without your positive advantage, the distinct, polarised group of differences for choosing you, you will have to fight it out on price comparisons and discounts at the bottom or if you are lucky, in the middle of the market place. You will appear beige and look like everyone else having to rely on volume sales to make your living. But a positive advantage will create a desire for you that is head and shoulders above the pack, permitting you to sell your signature wedding experience at the price you want because of the scarcity you'll be able to create. Signature wedding experiences that are scarce will always command higher prices due to limited supply. Creating your positive advantage will be one of the cornerstone secrets to your success and is something I push my students and challenge them with much deeper through my one-to-one mentoring sessions and online teaching programs. By definition your positive advantage will not be easy to attain, and because of the challenges faced when creating them, few wedding professionals see them through to completion, and deny themselves of the associated benefits. But I believe you are different, it can be done. I have crafted out a positive advantage for myself and I am helping others to do so for themselves as well. I believe that what one man or woman has done, another man or woman can do and that includes you. Believe in you as I do.

Wedding Marketing Mastery Challenge:

Go create your own positive advantage based on excellence, your brand, and ability to over-deliver. Expect hard work and hurdles but stay the course and hold onto your vision during the tough times. Remember, smart hard work resulting in the creation of a positive advantage, will help attract pre-sold ideal clients to you.

THE THIRD HABIT

Plan What Action You Need To Implement Right Now To Hit Your 3 Year Income, Lifestyle And Freedom Goals

In this step you will discover why you are not hitting your targets. You will also discover the steps and changes you must make in your life in order to reach your long term goals; those achievements that cannot be achieved today or tomorrow, nor next month, I'm referring to your big desires that require the passage of time for their attainment, for example you may want:

1. *70 bookings a year at your full rate.*

2. *A tripling of your fees from where they are today..*

3. *Have 50, 4 or 5 star wedding venue's listing you as a preferred supplier to give you an abundance of avatar's to choose from, and the luxury of being able to say "Sorry, I am already booked.".*

4. *To generate an annual income ahead of your financial needs giving you the financial freedom to live life on your own terms and to be able to help others, and avoid the effects of the feast/ famine cycle.*

5. *To be the authority in your industry, the natural go-to person whenever brides or venue's think of your category.*

Let's begin with that end in mind by identifying what your 3 year plan is. To get really clear use a 3 step mind map formula to get there.

Mind map step 1: What is your why?

List your emotional reasons for getting out of bed daily to do what you do. Go deep, pull out the meaningful emotional juice that will motivate and remind you of the purpose of your efforts whenever your journey gets gritty. For example you may write:

1. *I want to live my life at the highest level possible.*

2. *I want financial freedom to be able to help my parents, family and close friends.*

3. *I want to be able to make a difference through charitable donations to causes that are meaningful to me etc.*

Mind map trigger 1: Write down your own personal whys in the space below, remember to get as clear and as emotionally motivated as possible, add more whys on a separate page if you think of more than 5:

1 _____
_____
_____
_____

2 _____
_____
_____
_____

3 _____
_____
_____
_____

4 _____
_____
_____
_____

5 _____
_____
_____
_____

Mind map step 2: What are your financial desires?

List the material things you desire in your life, be as detailed as possible. It is critical that you place a cost beside each desire to give you a precise amount to aim for, for example you may write over 3 years I will need:

1. *£600,000 to become mortgage free*

2. *£108,000 for business and personal expenses*

3. *£72,000 to enjoy life's pleasures such as holidays, dinners, weekend breaks, provide family assistance, kids school / higher education fees, theatre, club memberships etc*

4. *£116,000 for property investments.*

In this example you would need:

£896,000 in total over the next 3 years. Your desires maybe higher or lower, but whatever they are, my recommendation would be to increase your total by a third (x1.3) to take account of unexpected expenses. In this case it would be £896,000 x 1.3 = £1,164,800

Which equates to:

£388,267 per year (above divided by 3), or

£32,356 per month (above divided by 12), or

£1,471 per day (above divided by 22 because I am assuming you will only want to work 22 days per month creating time to enjoy life with your friends and family).

The bigger your dreams and daily focus towards their attainment, the greater your chances of success. What are your dreams? Think big.

By way of a disclaimer, I am not a qualified financial advisor so please consult your FA before putting your plan into place. The purpose of this exercise is to motivate you into getting financial clarity on your money goals.

Mind map trigger 2: Write your huge audacious 'I wish I had' financial targets over the next 3 years in the space below, get really clear, include costs next to each desire and add more financial targets on a separate page if you have more than 5:

1 £_____ *Required to* _____

_____

_____

_____

2 £_____ *Required to* _____

_____

_____

_____

3 £_____ *Required to* _____

_____

_____

_____

4 £_____ *Required to* _____

_____

_____

_____

5 £_____ *Required to* _____

_____

_____

_____

Now fill in your totals below:

£ _____   Total money goal over 3 years

£ _____   x 1.3 for 30% buffer

£ _____   ÷ by 3 for your 3 year target

£ _____   ÷ above by 12 for your 1 year target

£ _____   ÷ above by 22 for your monthly target

It must be said, for a rounded life it is important for you to also acknowledge your psychological, spiritual, health, family, social and intimate needs. It is only for the sake of brevity you should concentrate on your financial needs for now. But please remember to detail your other needs at a later time in order for you enjoy a fuller, multi-dimensional life.

Mind map step 3: **What opportunities can you visualise to create lasting wealth?**

Write down the business ideas you have that are capable of accumulating the funds you require to achieve your huge audacious 'I wish I had' financial targets. Drill down to the numbers, this is very important for your daily focus. The more you focus on the detail and clarity of each goal and the more you 'see it' the better. Avoid wishy, washy statements, they won't serve you and will never be realised. Your goal should be very specific for example:

An opportunity yet to be realised in the next 12 months is to get 50, 4* or 5* wedding venue's to list me as a preferred supplier, generating an extra 36 bookings a year at £1,500 per booking. This will increase turnover by £54,000 each year totalling £162,000 over 3 years.

Mind map trigger 3: Complete these sentences:

My **first** business opportunity yet to be realised is:

_____

_____

_____

This will generate an extra £ .... over 12 months, and
£ .... over 3 years.

My **second** business opportunity yet to be realised is:

_____

_____

_____

This will generate an extra £ .... over 12 months, and
£ .... over 3 years.

My **third** business opportunity yet to be realised is:

_____

_____

_____

This will generate an extra £ .... over 12 months, and
£ .... over 3 years.

My **fourth** business opportunity yet to be realised is:

_____

_____

_____

This will generate an extra £ .... over 12 months, and
£ .... over 3 years.

My **fifth** business opportunity yet to be realised is:

_____

_____

_____

This will generate an extra £ .... over 12 months, and
£ .... over 3 years.

If you can think of more than 5 business opportunities please list them on a separate piece of paper.

Let's sum it up:

Total 3 year income from my opportunities. (Note this figure must equate to the 3 year figure that you completed in mind map 2.)

Finally, you must put an exact date next to your huge audacious 'I wish I had' financial targets and tie yourself to it starting today.

I want you to write:
I will achieve all 3 elements of my mind map by

(enter today's date plus 3 years).

I know if I can get you to take immediate action that becomes a daily habit you are more likely to follow through, so using your smartphone, take a photo of your mind map right now; begin each morning by reading it out aloud. Do the same each night before you retire to bed. This may sound strange but extensive studies have proven there are definite psychological benefits to you repeating your affirmations in this way, because you get that which you focus upon.

Your income is set by what you do daily

Remember the effect John C. Maxwell's quote had on me? I'm hoping that by completing the following exercise, it can help you as well.

In the 'activity' column on the table on the next page, list your typical daily routine. To get the most value and insight from this exercise, it is essential that you are completely honest and open about what it is you do with your time, for example, if you are:

- *Waking at 7.00am.*

- *Opening emails at 8.00am.*

- *Doing the school run at around 8.15am and 3.00pm.*

- *Speaking to potential clients around 4.00pm.*

- *On Facebook hourly.*

Put ink to paper and list your daily habits truthfully in the activity column. Remember these are things you would do on a typical day when you are not at a wedding – assuming that is, your profession requires you to actively be onsite. Take 10 minutes, do it now.

Exercise: List your daily routine

Time	Activity
5.00am	
6.00am	
7.00am	
8.00am	
9.00am	
10.00am	
11.00am	
12.00pm	
1.00pm	
2.00pm	
3.00pm	
4.00pm	
5.00pm	
6.00pm	
7.00pm	
8.00pm	
9.00pm	

Now imagine you had a magic diamond wedding ring, on rubbing it your Genie appears and says, *"I'm giving you one wish and one wish only - I will do anything you ask for to grow your wedding business beyond your wildest dreams. Ask it of me right now, and it shall be done..."*

Take a couple of minutes to think about The One Thing you would like your Genie to do that would completely transform your wedding business and your life, then write down what you would wish for in the space below. Once done please bookmark pages 37 and 38 for easy reference as you will need to refer to them again 3 times in future.

We'll come back to your answer soon, but for now, I'd like to share with you an important lesson I learnt during my 16 year career working for Legal & General Investment Management.

The firm employed over 230 members of staff spanning 3 floors across several departments including the Trading and Settlement Desks, Finance, Taxation, HR, Administration, Secretarial, Compliance, Administration, Systems, Banking, Performance Measurement and many more.

At the time I loved my job and corporate life. I busied myself socially in the company and made friends with many colleagues. But the big lesson I learnt and want to share with you was that the key directors ranked 3 departments more importantly than any other, and they were:

- *Marketing*

- *Sales*

- *Innovation* - the minds responsible for dreaming up new sought-after financial products and services to offer the market place tomorrow.

The reason was simple, these 3 departments were the only teams capable of attracting new business.

Even though the other departments, mine included, were essential to the to the smooth running of the firm, and we all had to perform competitively to retain clients, I learnt that we were spokes in the wheel that kept the business rolling but the wheel only grew through the promotional and campaigning efforts of the 3 departments bulleted above.

Your takeaway is, if you do not already identify a marketing, sales and innovation department within your wedding business, take immediate action to set them up now; but of more importance, manage your time to spend at least 51% of your typical business day working in marketing, sales or innovation if you want the fastest route to growth.

What each department should do

Marketing – Send really clear messages to your avatar that creates awareness for and magnetising desire to your wedding business.

Sales – Articulating value and conveying worth so effectively that your avatar buys your wedding experience.

As the owner of your business, you must excel in both marketing and sales. If you cannot do both, you will create cashflow problems for your company which in turn will adversely affect your personal life and ability to take care of yourself and those that depend on you.

Red Flag

If you know you cannot market or sell well you will never truly thrive. If this speaks to you it is quintessential to the success of your business and attainment of your 3 year goals that you get professionally trained. If you know this is something you've been thinking about for some time, take immediate action. Remember, never let procrastination prevent you from achieving your dream.

Innovation - If you offer the same product or service for long enough you will eventually become stale, and lose market share as innovative competitors eventually overtake you.

Learn to reinvent and refresh your signature wedding experience periodically if you want to become and remain the market leader.

THE FOURTH HABIT

Know When To Zone-In And Zone-Out

Thrive
ZONE 1

*Marketing, Sales
and Future
Innovation*

@ least 51% of your time daily

Labour
ZONE 2

*Office Work,
Delivering your
Niche and
Learning*

Lifestyle
ZONE 3

*Family, Friends
Pleasure
and Fun*

Thrive - Zone 1:

Marketing, Sales and Innovation

Success in business leaves clues, and your takeaway from this section is in knowing that your Marketing, Sales and Innovation activities are the only ways to make your business thrive. Your second takeaway is to change (if necessary) so you spend at least 51% of your business day immersed in the Thrive Zone if you are serious about growing your business.

Examples of activities in the Thrive - Zone 1 include:

- *Telephoning potential brides*
- *Pitching an avatar*
- *Networking with other wedding creatives*
- *Getting on the preferred list of 4* and 5*wedding venue's*
- *Dominating the first page of Google for the keywords you want to be found for*
- *Buying leads from wedding directories*
- *Creating a fanbase on Facebook, Twitter and LinkedIn*
- *List building*
- *Attending wedding fairs*
- *Word-of-mouth recommendations*
- *Having a professionally designed website*
- *Direct marketing via post*
- *Inventing desirable, new and difficult-to-duplicate wedding experiences to keep you ahead of your competition.*

I remember running my first company on quitting Legal & General Investment Management; during that spell I had no real understanding of the importance of devoting at least 51% of each business day to the Thrive – Zone 1 activities. I ran a start-up from home and had no office at the time so I used our ironing board as a desk which I set up in our small double bedroom, perching on the end of the chair I took from the family dining table, I spent hours and hours going over the company accounts and other boring administrative tasks. I was busy being busy working on the various papers spread across the ironing board tapping away at my laptop, thinking I was growing a business. And whilst those tasks were important to keeping my company up-to-date and operational they did nothing to directly drive ideal clients to my order book. I had no strategy for success, I just worked hard and for long hours on everything because it made me feel like I was moving forward, but really I was without direction. Has this ever happened to you?

It was at a time when I had not yet discovered the importance of 'The Money Hours' - those golden moments in the day when your avatar is most likely to welcome contact from you, the hours you should block out to make contact with your prospects, and by 'block out' I mean shut down email, Facebook, notifications and all other distractions whilst you focus and conquer the task in hand. So before we move on, let's discover what the Money Hours are for your avatar by filling in the blanks in the following sentence completion exercise:

1. *My avatar is more likely to take my call during her lunch break between _____ and _____ .*

2. *My avatar may have an afternoon break at _____ when there is a slim chance I may be able to reach her.*

3. *A better time to reach out to my avatar will be on her commute home and before dinner between _____ and _____ .*

4. *Another opportunity to call is just after dinner between _____ and _____ .*

5. *Unless I have gained advance permission, I will never call my avatar after _____ because I consider this to be her personal time to spend with her family or partner.*

6. *The prime time to reach my avatar could be over the weekend between _____ and _____ .*

7. *The worst time to reach out to my avatar is probably on a _____ day morning between _____ and _____ , because she's likely to be immersed in work.*

It's time to reflect, take another look at the exercise you completed on page 37, under the heading *'List your daily routine'*. It's on the section I asked you to bookmark. Thumb back and glance down at what you are currently trading your Money Hours for daily, then look again at the sentences you have just completed. If in this moment you realise you are mis-using your Money Hours, precious seconds you will never get back in exchange for something else, this is your wake-up call to change.

Put another way, it's like getting to the peak period in your Money Hours and putting a sign on your desk that has your full name in bold with the title Marketing, Sales and Innovative Director underneath it followed by the message: *"I am away from my desk at the moment because I have chosen not to grow my business at peak times, I'll be back later, sorry for any inconvenience."*

Red Flag

Metaphorically speaking, the next time you are about to 'put' that sign on your desk during your Money Hours ask yourself this question: "Is what I am I am about to do right now more important than ensuring the growth of my business?"

I know you lead a busy life and you find it difficult to squeeze everything in, but it's vital for the long-term success of your business that you spend prime time creating an environment in which your business can thrive and that's by being in Zone 1, because the longer that sign remains on your desk during your Money Hours, the longer it will take to turn your business around.

If this resonates ask yourself *"What simple changes can I make right now to carry out more activities capable of making my business thrive at peak times?"*

Earlier in Habit 3, I asked what would you like your Genie to do for you. (you bookmarked it on page 38.) Please re-write your answer below:

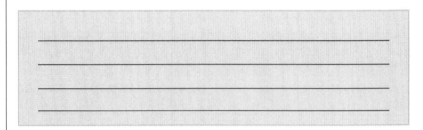

I'm guessing you wrote a Thrive – Zone 1 activity right?! Truth is you probably already know what to do to magnify your wedding business, you just need a little guidance on how to increase the intensity, frequency and consistency of your activities.

Labour – Zone 2:

Office work, delivering your signature wedding experience and Learning

View Zone 2 as 'The Glue' to your wedding business, the activities responsible for the smooth running of your niche. Labour – Zone 2 activities are time consuming, essential but generate no direct income.

The activities under the Labour - Zone 2 umbrella include:

- *Submitting accounts*
- *Order fulfilment on the day of the wedding*
- *Administration*
- *Deliveries and collections*
- *Education*
- *Office cleaning*
- *Travel*

In fact the Labour – Zone 2 remit is so enormous it covers everything to do with the running of your wedding business outside of Thrive – Zone 1.

How to minimise time in Labour - Zone 2, so you can immerse yourself in Thrive – Zone 1

1. Whenever possible, relegate Zone 2 (and Zone 3) activities outside of your 'Money Hours'. Especially if you are the only employee in your business.

2. Delegate everything you find yourself repeating. Because these are the trainable activities which could be performed by someone else, you have much more important work to immerse yourself in by growing your company and this is done by immersing yourself in Thrive - Zone 1. If you have staff in your business, learn to let go and delegate as many Labour - Zone 2 activities as you can. You might be in the same position that I am in, i.e. the only person in your company with no-one to delegate to. In this case outsource tasks on a case by case basis whenever the opportunity arises. My partner Julie is incredibly supportive of my wedding businesses, has accurate accounting skills and takes care of my books for me. Is there someone supportive who you can lean on to manage parts of your business? Outside of friends and family I have outsourced work to resources like Fiverr and People Per Hour, sourced skilled people on LinkedIn. You do not have to hire a full time team, I never have. Fill your skills gap as and when you need to, let Google become your HR department, or ask for advice from peers who faced and overcame similar short term staffing challenges.

3. STOP DOING IT MANUALLY. I am astonished at the number of wedding professionals who still respond to purchased wedding leads, wedding fair enquiries, online requests or telephone messages by manually amending a self-made email template. If this speaks to you take note and take action. There is a faster, more accurate way of dealing with avatar enquiries. With just a few keystrokes by you or a staff member, an email system can take over and handle all your initial enquiries and all follow-ups virtually AUTOMATICALLY eating up this time hungry Labour – Zone 2 activity with ease. It's called a Client Relationship Management system, also known as a CRM.

Today CRM's can be set-up with starting prices around the £10pm mark. Can you imagine paying a member of staff a tenner a month to work for you 24/7, 365? Someone who never calls in sick or forgets to send out important emails? Someone who always sends your marketing and sales messages out right on time, handling umpteen response permutations simultaneously depending how far down your sales funnel your avatar has travelled? I cannot tell you how many thousands of emails my CRM has sent out for me in fact without it, I would not have a wedding business, I'd have an administrating business.

If you do not have a CRM and you plan to grow your wedding business get one. You need one. Take action and do it now, even if you are small at the moment – because it will set you up for good habits when you expand. A good CRM will be able to handle all your customer relationships far better than your manual time consuming system ever could. From contact information to venue location, to booking agreements, invoicing, thank-you notes, and so much more. It will breeze through virtually everything repetitively administrative relating to the servicing of your clients from beginning to end, all in one place and accessible using secure login credentials from any computer in the world with an internet connection.

Since getting my own CRM I feel like I have an efficient, administration manager taking care of virtually all my repetitive email follow-ups, freeing my time for Thrive – Zone 1 activities for a minute fraction of the cost of employing someone. I go deeper into CRM later on in this book but for now, just know that it is essential to the growth of your business that you get one. The CRM I use is called DJ Event Planner and it is available as a download online. Do not think this is an exclusive DJ tool because of the name, it is not. It is a very powerful event planning system and can be used by wedding professionals across the board. By way of full disclosure: it is a bit technical and I have hit roadblocks setting it up, furthermore support can be slow coming, but once up and running this CRM was a game changer for me. If you prefer to source you own CRM there is a massive pool to choose from, do your own due diligence but know this, you must have one in your tool box to reduce your Labour – Zone 2 workload which at times can feel like pushing treacle uphill.

Lifestyle – Zone 3:

Family, Friends, Pleasure, and Fun

Lifestyle – Zone 3 activities are pleasurable pastimes that make you feel amazing temporarily but produce nothing towards your goal of attracting and booking higher paying brides. As the saying goes: you can pay now and play later, or play now and pay later but either way, one day, you will pay.

Lifestyle – Zone 3 activities embrace all the fun things in life including: holidays, theatre trips, parties, bar-b-cues, socialising with friends and family, love, sex, retail therapy, long weekends, spa sessions, lunches, gym, Facebook, (the non business side), TV entertainment shows, concerts, live games, dinners, dancing and all other pastimes that fill you with the feel good factor.

There have been moments in my career when I have over indulged in Lifestyle - Zone 3 activities for the most part of an entire day. As a self-employed entrepreneur, I am answerable only to myself, family and friends and the demands of my monthly outgoings, so in theory I can do what I like when I like. And so can you. This is one of the benefits of us both not working a J.O.B. (Just Over Broke) but it requires a great deal of self-discipline not to over extend time in Lifestyle - Zone 3, especially when you still need to grow your wedding business and produce income for yourself and for those you love and care for. Remember there will always be a price to pay for over indulging in Lifestyle - Zone 3 activities, for me it often meant working way into the small hours of the night to catch up.

There was also a period in my life to my deepest regret when I slaved at my desk for up to 16 hours a day to make ends meet. My kids who were much younger at the time would bound excitedly into the office I eventually set-up at home wanting to play after school, but I would send them out choosing instead to overwork. I failed to make time, instead I needed to make money, my family's financial survival depended upon it. But here's the thing, if I could go back in time I would spend much of it sharing Lifestyle - Zone 3 moments with my children, I would attend more school plays instead of the token few during their early years. I would take time out each evening to play with them. I would read more bedtime stories to them and teach them more things as their father. If not me, who? I was wrong to see them as a noisy distraction to my goals. One of my most painful moments was having to miss my daughter Ella's 16 birthday party due to work. The brown envelopes were piling up on my desk, many still unopened when a last minute offer for work came in and although it was low paying, in my desperation I took it because I knew it would ease my family's financial struggle; but in so doing I missed one of the most precious celebrations in my daughter's life. Precious moments I could never get back... I now hold the unshakeable belief that my partner Julie, our children, my mother and closest friends and family are the most important and precious people in the world to me but success without them in my life would mean very little. If you can relate to a thread of my personal story, and it serves to help you avoid repeating the errors of my ways, then sharing and disclosing with you will have been worth it.

Today I work very hard and very smart and I play that way to. I believe both you and I should purposefully and very deliberately plan Lifestyle - Zone 3 activities to spend time with the people that mean the most to us and to celebrate the lives God has blessed us with.

Lifestyle - Zone 3 activities are there to refresh, replenish and enrich; by creating moments of joy for self and others. If there is one thing you takeaway from these lines it's to avoid the trap of spending your entire life working in Thrive - Zone 1 and Labour - Zone 2 exclusively. I know of no one who on their deathbed wished they spent more time at work, in fact in the moments you think your life will end your final thoughts will be of those closest to you. Let me share another personal story and you will see more clearly why I know this to be true...

I was driving back from Leigh and Brad's wedding held at The Shenley Cricket Centre in Hertfordshire. Their amazing celebration of love finished at midnight on Thursday 10 July, 2014 but by the time I had packed down and set off home to my children in South Woodham Ferrers, Essex, it was just after 1.00am.

As I drove home in the dead of the night I thought back over the inner glow Leigh and Brad radiated that day. I felt proud to have contributed my small part towards the success of one of the happiest days of their lives. I felt good, even if a little tired.

Whilst travelling anti-clockwise around the M25 I momentarily lost concentration, I looked back at the road but I knew it was already too late. Impact at speed into the car that had suddenly stopped in front of me was as inexorable as death. I had just a matter of seconds. I was in the outside lane. The central reservation to my right and cars to my left all blurred past as my car sped forward into the ever decreasing space. I remember the blackness of the night warmed by the glow of the yellow/orangish street lights above. I remember a bridge. I thought this is it. I trod hard on the brakes but in that moment I knew there was not enough stopping distance between my screeching wheels and the black car I was rushing toward too fast, closer and closer, collision was certain. I yelled out loud "God! Noooo!" I was too young and not ready to die. I had so much to do, to give.

About a year earlier my marriage had irretrievably broken down and at the time of my accident I was alone and had not yet found Julie, the amazing new love of my life and so in those last nano seconds I thought only of the very closest loved ones to me, my 4 children. The urgency and emergency of my pending crash slowed down time frame by frame, but my thought process speeded up... "I've not yet done enough for my children.... Who will provide for them?" My last thought was deep disappointment. "They will not be able to go on the mini holiday we were looking forward to in Disneyland Paris"...

Crash. I blacked out.

When I came to, thin pixilated smoke was already clearing caused by the detonation of both airbags creating a pungent odour in the cabin. "Why can't I see clearly?" The impact from the driver airbag had knocked the glasses from my face, I fished around for the spare pair I kept in the drivers door and put them on. "Oh, my God, what about the people I hit, please God, let them be OK". I got out the car and luckily, very luckily, everyone involved in the accident walked away with nothing more than bruises but this was my personal wake-up call to create a new balanced life with my second chance. To love and celebrate life in Lifestyle - Zone 3 as much as possible, simultaneously providing for those I care for and myself.

When we are faced with the reality of our own mortality, you and I won't be thinking of work, we will think of those we love. It's true Lifestyle - Zone 3 activities will not add a penny to your bank account but they will build up massive reserves in your emotional bank account. Remember to always make time for close friends and family, in the end they will be all you have.

Are You Zoning-In Daily On The Right Activities?

For the final time, thumb back to the daily activities you bookmarked on page 37.

1. *Take a look at the Daily Activities you entered in Habit 3*

2. *Look down your daily activities timeline from 5.00am to 9.00pm and count up the number of Thrive – Zone 1 activities you listed each hour on a typical day.*

3. *If you counted 2 Thrive – Zone 1 activities put the number 2 in the Thrive – Zone 1 illustration below.*

4. *Repeat this process for labour – Zones 2, and Lifestyle – Zone 3.*

Thrive
ZONE 1

Marketing, Sales and Future Innovation

From Habit 3, I recorded that I create

THRIVE hours each day to

Labour
ZONE 2

Office Work, Delivering your Niche and Learning

From Habit 3, I recorded that I immerse myself

hours each day
LABOURING

Lifestyle
ZONE 3

Family, Friends Pleasure and Fun

From Habit 3, I recorded that I spend

hours each day
LIFESTYLING

Moment of Truth: Your wedding business will reap monthly what you sow hourly

Red Flag

Reflect, take a long hard look at the sum of your current daily habits because you are looking at the quantity and quality of oxygen you are breathing in your wedding business.

Are you sowing enough seeds hourly to allow your wedding business to thrive, or are you in danger of choking off any hope of reaching out to the prospects all around you in a way that would make an impact on your life and the lives of the people you love and care for?

On analysing where you are right now do you need to zone into Thrive – Zone 1 much more often? Are you short-changing your business of its Marketing, Sales and Innovation Director? If you are not running those departments vigorously, who will? And by vigorously, I mean spending at least 51% of your time daily, (outside of being at a wedding).

You can either do this on your own by leveraging the knowledge gained from The 12 Habits thus far, or you can join my 1-1 mentoring program and learn how to attract and book brides who decide on value not price. Neil Johnson is a great case study: With guidance, Neil was able to double his fee, paving the way for him to leave his day job in order to become a wedding creative. If you don't want to walk the walk alone, discover the fastest and most direct path to success by visiting:

www.weddingmarketingmastery.co.uk

THE FIFTH HABIT

Articulate Value Before Giving A Price

When you offer premium wedding experiences at high prices, the one question you do not want asked within the first few minutes of an initial enquiry is "How much do you cost?" Answer this question too early and there is a very high chance you'll never hear from your prospect again, but answer that same question after you've created the opportunity to explain your value, unique differences and the passion you have for your work and you'll significantly increase the possibility of converting that prospect into a high paying client.

Why is this?

The majority of couples have never planned a wedding before, and although some hire wedding planners or take other professional advice, most attempt to figure out the wedding planning process on their own, from friends and family, or via Google. It is a massive undertaking for them and bearing in mind they will probably book around 20 or so individual wedding suppliers and it takes anywhere between 7 to 12 points of contact per supplier before a booking decision is made, it's very easy to understand how overwhelming and time consuming it is for a couple. They are unlikely to be experts in your field and so won't have much else to ask, so they often use price (at least in the early stages) to shortlist wedding creatives until they've gained a better understanding of their options. If we think about it, couples phone around so they can slowly build up knowledge about their supplier options and eventually settle on those which they like and believe can deliver what they need. At the initial enquiry stage, although they may ask you for a price, what most really want is information about the experience you offer to help them gain the confidence that you can solve their problem which is to find a brilliant photographer, venue, caterer, car firm or whatever wedding supplier category they need.

Why price shopping alone could be flawed

Example 1.

Let's assume you are a florist and a bouquet of your top flowers cost £135, and a competitor, a few yards down the street charges a discounted price of £35 for a bouquet of similar looking flowers. On price alone the bride may think "Hey I can save £100 per bunch by buying the cheaper flowers". The thing is, there are reasons for the price differentials which only become apparent through Q & A, which is why, in this case, a meeting would be enlightening:

- *Your flowers are grown in your exclusive gardens and are one-off limited editions, the cheaper flowers are mass produced in several locations and are widely available.*

- *Your flowers are allowed to grow organically over a natural period of time whilst the cheap flowers are speed produced with the aid of growth chemicals and pesticides.*

- *In full bloom, your flowers look vibrantly alive, effuse a beautiful aroma and look enriched whilst the budget flowers by comparison smell ordinary, present an uneven colour and appear simple and much less presentable.*

- *Because of the way your flowers are grown they last longer after cutting, but the cheap ones soon wilt.*

Compared on price alone the cheap flowers would save the bride a fistful of pounds but in this case, price has not revealed the full picture. And if the bride met you and you were able to tell her about the extra value and differences linked to your flowers versus the cheaper ones, do you think she may buy from you instead? Especially if by asking questions you found out that:

1. *It was important to the bride to have unique organic flowers because she deeply believed in reducing toxic chemical usage.*

2. *She was concerned about the ozone depletion.*

3. *A beautiful deep aroma was very important to her.*

4. *The bride wanted to give them away after the wedding to close elderly relatives and she wanted them to last as long as possible.*

By inviting her to your store the bride will be able to experience and visualise how her venue will look in a much more persuasive and influential way than would be impossible by phone. You and I both know that weddings are emotional not logical purchases, and you'd be able to place her in an emotional state allowing the bride to see, feel, smell and touch for herself how your flowers would match her needs perfectly. So when all is said and done, which flowers do you think the bride will end up buying now that she is able to make a better informed decision? The art of marketing and sales is offering influential and persuasive information articulated in a way that resonates with your avatar. Learn to do this masterfully and you will never be without brides wanting to book you.

By definition, price is never at the top of the list of deciding factors governing the buying decisions of discerning higher paying couple's. Factors like quality, hiring expert industry leaders, certainty of perfection, luxury, impressive outcomes are. Don't get me wrong price is important but it is never number one. Never. Higher paying brides and grooms buy on emotions, wants and feelings, rarely logic and if your wedding experience aligns with her desires your avatar will pay what it takes to secure you. It's down to your marketing and sales skills to ensure the matchmaking that ties the knot.

So how do you get the bride to meet you so you can explain what your USPs are?

If you operate at the high-end, it is essential for you to develop the art of price deflection until you've had an opportunity to explain your value first if you want to increase your conversion rate.

Ask for the meeting, but explain why you want one. Create a captivating message that grabs the attention of your couple, heightens desire for your signature wedding experience and gives them just enough to excite a keen interest in you but leaves them wanting to meet you to discover more.

If you struggle articulating this in an email I've written a free fill-in-the-blank template called 'How To Focus A Brides Attention On Value Not Price' and you can download it here:

www.weddingmarketingmastery.co.uk/blog

THE SIXTH HABIT

Apply The 7 Influencers And Powers Of Persuasion To Convert Prospects Into Clients

Can you imagine what it would feel like to go into every meeting knowing your service level and communication skills were so powerful and magnetic, that couples nearly always booked you?

Having met the prerequisite of creating a positive advantage, what would it do for your confidence if you were able to articulate value and convey worth so well, that your avatar nearly always booked you at your premium price?

How relaxed would you feel going into a meeting fluent in a language that resonated with your avatar? A language few of your competitors could speak.

What follows are the 7 influencers and powers of persuasion that I use throughout my own presentations that are so effective 8 out of 10 prospects book me at premium rates. Master them, make them your own and there is no reason why they can't do the same for you.

1. In order to influence you must first be influenced

Success happens in your mind long before it materialises in your business. Believe in yourself even when others tell you to let go of your dream.

It will be those closest to you who will tell you "It can't be done." Quite often these are the people who care about you the most and want to protect you from the pain of possible failure but have ironically never stood in the shoes of failure nor success in your pursuit, and whenever you experience similar unqualified opinions you should ask the same question I silently ask myself whenever others try to derail my dreams and that is "Does your life experience and track record qualify you to make such a judgement that if I follow, will kill off the very chance of my success?" I often also think of this famous Henry Ford quote:

"The man who thinks he can and the man who thinks he can't are both right."

You see, both empowering and limiting beliefs have the capacity to deliver their package. Which is why you should set your mindset very carefully.

Within your own business, you will meet dream makers and dream takers. As long as you have the talent, the ability to carve out a positive advantage and an unshakeable self-belief, hold onto your vision and let no one tear it away from you ever. If you want high paying couples to believe in you, you must first believe in yourself.

Self-belief enhanced by a positive advantage were the game-changers that eventually created a demand for my services way in excess of my ability to deliver. Now I turn away more couples than ever due to existing bookings. I feel a little self-conscious telling you this especially when I know so many struggle to get booked regularly, but I sincerely tell you this from a point of gratefulness that I found a path to proven success that I am now able to share with you. Success is replicable through a step by step process. The 7 influencers I will share with you in this section form part of it. They made a huge difference to my wedding business and have the capacity to make a huge difference to yours.

Self Motivation:

5 ways in which I can upscale my self-belief are:

1 _____

2 _____

3 _____

4 _____

5 _____

2. Trigger the Law of Reciprocity by Giving Away Something Free

Your free gift must move the needle and add value to your couples wedding planning process. Period.

If your gift is token or does not propel them into a genuine state of gratitude you will be wasting your time and potentially cheapening your brand. Equally, your free gift must be of low monetary cost to you for obvious reasons but of high appreciative value to your prospects.

Your free gift should also double up as a way to build your expert glow and increase your likability factor. One way to keep all these plates spinning is by sharing your expertise in a way that penetrates deeper than the level most of your competitors consider going to.

Think how much time you can save your couples from searching on Google for solutions simply by telling them the answers to the typical wedding challenges they face. For example, engaged couples have little idea of the timeline for their wedding whilst they are in the early supplier hiring stages, but as an expert in your field, you do. No matter what your speciality is you could create a customised timeline for your prospects from the beginning until the end of their wedding day, then share that information with them offering guidance through it.

I can tell you it works amazingly! I have had so many comments about this strategy. This is an extract from an email Stephanie and Ben sent me the day after we met:

"Hi Terry,
Thank you so much for your time today, it was a pleasure to meet you and so useful to have someone actually explain to us the timeline of the day and the little bits that we wouldn't have thought about!..."

The longer you have been in the wedding industry the more likely it is you may suffer from 'Expert Obviousness' and think this is way too simplistic, and that everybody knows it because it has become ingrained within you through constant repetition but the reality is this stuff is like manna falling from heaven to your prospects, because they are still trying to figure it out and often nobody is showing it to them at the time of your meeting!

I know this to be true from first-hand experience, because post meeting, couples leave me feeling elated, enthusiastic and empowered about their day simply because I shared useful and valuable information that brought their wedding to life and relieved some of the stress of the unknown.

By ensuring you always leave prospects being able to visualise their day with more clarity and discover new ideas they had not thought of, fuelled with excitement and enthusiasm, they will leave viewing you as their expert; and experts who are liked and trusted get booked.

Be Sticky

Creating an expert glow is one of the factors capable of driving up an increased demand for your services, and if you can choreograph your meetings to ensure your brides and grooms leave feeling thrilled, you'll motivate them to hold you as the benchmark compared to other suppliers, and compel them to return after looking around because they found no one better and that's called being 'Sticky'. How 'Sticky' are you right now? Triggering the law of reciprocity is one way to increase your draw.

Giving a valuable free gift that creates a thankful feeling within your prospect triggers the law of reciprocity, the power of which increases in line with the perceived value of your free gift or gifts. The recipient may even want to repay you in some way for your act of kindness.

But this should not be your only reason for sharing wedding intel. Doing a good deed by navigating a couple through their day is rewarding enough.

Just think about the last time somebody gave you a helpful, relevant, valuable gift that you were not expecting, how did it make you feel? Did you want to give something back in return impulsively, even if it was just your thanks? I assure you, your prospects will bear your expert gift in mind when shortlisting. Anything that forces you to standout by being unique, passionate, helpful and likeable will motivate couples into booking you.

Self Motivation:

3 Valuable tips I could give away for free to heighten my perceived position as an expert in the eyes of my avatar and reduce their wedding planning pain points are:

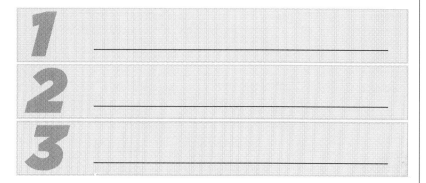

3. Be passionate about your craft

If there are 2 things higher paying brides love, they are passion and added value. Match and mirror the wants of your prospects by demonstrating a genuine excitement and passion for serving at their wedding, simultaneously exemplifying why you are the best in your field and watch your bride and groom draw closer and closer to booking you.

People buy passionate people and passion is contagious. When your couple realise your number one goal is to do whatever it takes to have them float away from their wedding feeling like nothing on earth could have gone better, getting booked gets easier.

Let me ask you a question: have you ever fallen in love with and purchased something even though a cheaper option was available? A car, holiday, item of clothing? Either choice would serve its purpose but you chose the dearer option over the cheaper choice because, you believed with a passion you'd gain more pleasure through buying the higher ticket option over the lower priced alternative.

In short you weighed up the added value you would gain by buying premium and it outweighed the extra cost, to the point that price was not an objection, in fact the cheapness and lesser quality of the alternative was. You were driven by emotion and you used logic to justify the higher spend. Always remember that premium brides are governed by this exact same buying criteria when considering you. Passion for the perfect solution relegates price off the top spot for discerning couples. You just need to articulately and passionately convey where you add value alongside your great benefits to ease prospects closer to conversion.

Selling high valued wedding experiences is easy

Have you ever been around someone who has just purchased something expensive? They are generally euphoric right? In fact they are so full of passion and pleasure the feeling has often been described as 'retail therapy'. Now view this from the wedding suppliers viewpoint, do you think they experienced 'hard work' whilst their prospect was passionately buying? Absolutely not... And I'm here to tell you that higher paying brides and grooms love to buy, but they hate to be sold. When you articulate the value of your wedding experience in a genuinely passionate way and portray caring, authority and expertise coupled with the talent to deliver a stellar service you go along way to creating a brand with a reputation for excellence and dependability, and it is at this point that you will come across as the natural solution and get the price you want to achieve. If you currently find it difficult to book your premium wedding experience it's likely the solution will be found in either:

1. *The way you communicate and walk prospects through your sales funnel*

2. *The wedding experience you offer needs altering to make it resonate more closely with your target audiences deepest desires, or*

3. *A combination of 1. and 2. above*

Self Motivation:
3 Ways I can demonstrate passion and articulate value are:

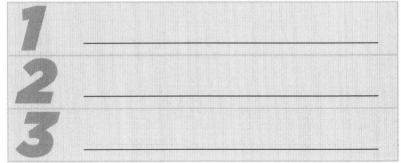

4. Position yourself as the expert, use your expertise and authority to prescribe never sell

The magnetic attraction of the expert glow.

Imagine you are taken seriously ill and find yourself in a backstreet doctors surgery. The specialist examining you seems quite unsure about your condition, regularly referring to medical books for confirmations throughout your examination. The surgery looks unprofessional and medical papers are strewn across cabinets. Post examination, the doctor eventually diagnoses XYZ and prescribes urgent and immediate surgery to prevent the inevitable spread and has a slot available that afternoon. Do you allow him to put you under general anaesthetic, wheel you through for your operation on a steel trolley and cut you open without so much as a second opinion? Based on your first impressions of him and the state of the surgery, probably not.

Imagine instead you find yourself in London Harley Street, where after being checked in by the smart uniformed receptionist, you notice medical certificates decorating the north wall of the waiting area. In a short while you are called through to the specialists surgery who confidently exams you, and upon completion, diagnosis you as suffering from XYZ, but to ensure there is no doubt he calls in another specialist for a second opinion who concurs. They both recommend urgent and immediate surgery to prevent the inevitable spread and they have an appointment open that afternoon. There is a much higher chance you'll make the call to your nearest and dearest, sign the consent form to allow them to take you through to theatre.

Identical prescriptions. Different opinions on the expertise of each medic. Different buying decisions. This is the magnetic attraction of the expert glow.

Now take a step back from your wedding business - when diagnosing the problems brides and grooms want solved through your wedding experience, do you ensure your marketing and sales funnels lead you to prescribe expert, compelling and irresistible solutions? Do this and couples will hire you more times than not. Fail and you will have to sell hard alongside the competition and sometimes discount in order to secure your bookings.

Mastery of the 12 Habits will eventually lead you to prescribe, not sell.

Self Motivation:

Step up and stand out.

5 hallmarks I can use to surround myself in a wedding expert glow that will be i) hard for me to attain and ii) almost impossible for my competitors to copy are:

(Note if none exist, list those that you are prepared to work hard at to create, because it is essential you have or acquire an expert glow or you will have to fight it out on price with the masses.)

5. Offer a money back guarantee

During my early teens I had no idea the American entrepreneur Victor Kiam would influence my marketing strategy decades later.

I was in the sitting room in my mother's council flat at 71 Bluebird Walk, Chalkhill Estate, Wembley during the 70's, watching our 14" black and white TV, when an advert came on and there was Victor Kiam confidently guaranteeing *"The Remington will shave you as close as a blade, or your money back!"*

I had not even hit puberty, yet the power of his confidence held my attention, I can only imagine the effect his promise had on his hairy target audience! His differences made Remington stand out against his competition, memorable to a pre-puberty schoolboy and contributed to the massive success of his company.

Some time in the small hours of 2012 I was restless and could not sleep, I can only assume I was worried about the bills and still lying in bed with the bedside light on, I flashed back to Victor Kiam's TV advert, and in that moment decided to differentiate my wedding business. I would guarantee my brides and grooms *"You will love everything I'll do for you or your money back."*

This powerful guarantee was the first differentiator I introduced. The shock and attention my message demanded instantly changed the way brides viewed me. It interrupts their patten and gets them to pay attention. At the time none of my competitors were doing this and even today, few do. The distinction gave my avatar a confidence in me that they were not getting elsewhere and contributed to me getting me more bookings at higher prices. I began to stand out. It marked the beginning of change.

Was I worried at first? Absolutely. Did anyone ever ask for a full refund? Never because I began each wedding with the end in mind that I would do everything in my power to ensure my couple would leave their wedding feeling emotionally fulfilled, and that nothing on earth could have gone better.

Offering a money-back guarantee is one of the most powerful Thrive – Zone 1 activities you can trigger to attract and book higher paying brides and one most of your rivals will shy away from out of fear of under delivering which is precisely why you should do it.

Yes, that's right, I'm advising you to create a money-back guarantee for your wedding business.

On reading this it is highly possible I've made you clench your buttocks so tightly, if you were sitting on a lump of coal it would be a diamond right now :) But seriously, if you have a highly desirable signature wedding experience that you passionately offer and you strive to over deliver on the aspirations of your ideal client, and enjoy the distinction of a 100% client satisfaction record, just do it. It will contribute to transforming your business, stamp trust all over your brand and be another elevating factor separating you from your competitors.

Need a bigger reason? Do you see your business as a market leader that's trustworthy confident and dependable? Think of your favourite world class company that matches this description (mine is Apple). What guarantee does the company you love offer? How does that guarantee make you feel when you purchase versus a company that does not?

Self Motivation:

Complete the following paragraph:

I have a 100% client satisfaction record to date and I often receive letters, cards, emails and social media expressions of deeply sincere thanks from couple's who have used my services. I want a Thrive - Zone 1 action that shocks and grabs the attention of high paying couple's to separate me further from my competitors and project an unrivalled confidence to my avatar that compels them at a minimum to short list me. This is why I will immediately introduce my money-back guarantee on: (enter todays date).

6. Social Proof Moves The Needle Of Your Business

Prospects expect you to say you are the best because they know you want their business so your affirmations of awesomeness will always fall on partially sceptical ears... at least initially.

The more prospects discover your wedding business being positively talked about by large numbers of brides, grooms, guests and wedding suppliers both on and offline, the better, so do everything you can to ignite this fire and keep it raging.

Reading moving testimonials by others who have used your services have the power to ease prospects another notch further down your sales funnel. It is for this reason whenever I present to couples at meetings, the penultimate slide before price disclosure is always an emphatic testimonial. Why? Hiring a wedding creative is an emotional, not logical decision and I want my bride and groom in a highly emotive state when I price reveal. Furthermore, I want someone else to do that job for me. Creating the belief you can deliver on a prospects expectations is one of the strongest influencers you can employ.

Terry's Top Tip:

Find your most moving testimonial and present it to prospects just before price revelation. This influencer is most effective when emphatically read out loud at face-to-face meetings.

Excellent places to showcase testimonials are on your website, Facebook and other social media channels. One of my favourite ways of using testimonials is via a silent conversation between past brides and prospects at face-to-face meetings just prior to getting into the meeting content.

I leave thank you letters and cards on my coffee table whilst I excuse myself to get refreshments, inviting my prospects to flick through the powerful testimonials whilst out of the room. This plays a small part in pre-selling and building the expert glow. Social proof is very influential in underpinning messages you put out, because when people are uncertain about what to do, more often than not they will follow the lead of others who've had a brilliant experience with you before.

High paying brides want to feel confident that you have done it before and that you can do it again. Third party social proof makes it easier for them to believe this about you.

Another powerful social endorser is to survey couples after each wedding. Ask them to rate you out of 10 in key areas of the overall experience you provided, then put your results into a table and feed it forward to prospective brides and grooms. The closer your scores are to 10, the more influential your survey will be. To minimise potential scepticism which some couples will have, use a trusted third party to independently collect your data for transparency. I have used the free tool by www.surveymonkey.com and found it more than suitable. I have also used independent surveys carried out on me by The Wedding Industry Awards.

Self Motivation:

4 Things I can do to encourage past clients, guests or wedding suppliers to talk positively about me on and offline are:

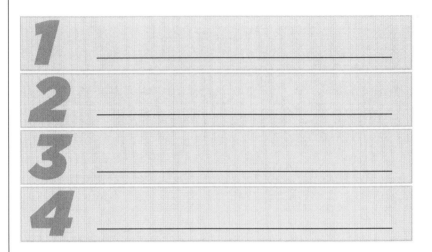

7. Be Scarce

If you are small enough to offer a signature wedding experience that can only be served to one couple per wedding day, use this to your advantage and turn limited availability into exclusivity. Let prospects know in a classy way that you can only do one wedding per day and if you have done a good enough job with the other 6 points above and they really like you, it will speed up their decision making process to hire you because they won't want to lose you to another couple.

In my own post follow-up email message I always conclude with the following passage because I want to highlight scarcity and ensure my limited availability is front of mind:

...AVAILABILITY

<first_name>, I am pleased to say I am currently available on <event_date_long>, and would love to provide you with a first class award winning service, but you should know that I take bookings on a first come first served basis and on average, I have to disappoint over 50 couples each year because by the time they've decided they want me, I've already been booked by another couple, so <first_name>

even though you have time and space to make a decision, please bear this in mind if you are leaning towards booking me...

Self Motivation:

3 Ways in which I can create a sense of scarcity to my advantage are:

Conclusion

On their own these 7 influencers are powerfully persuasive, but when combined they trigger a synergistic domino effect weighting buying decisions in your favour.

Not a client meeting goes by without me incorporating all of the 7 influencers because I know how powerfully persuasive they are in contributing to my 8 out of 10 conversion rate. In fact, now you understand what underpins my meetings, the next step is to show you my Keynote presentation deck which I'll cover in the next Habit. As you go through it, look out for the opportunities I purposefully create in which I weave in the 7 influencers and powers of persuasion. It will help you to discover a more powerful way of articulating and communicating your worth to your own couples.

If you meet with resistance to the idea of face-face meetings and you have never tried them before, know this: successful wedding businesses continuously try new marketing strategies and this is one I highly recommend you try to make your own. If the Keynote style turns out to be not your thing, I still recommend using the 7 influencers in the flow of your conversation to powerfully and ethically prescribe to your avatar.

In closing, your prospect's Keynote or Powerpoint presentation can be emailed to them after your meeting, leaving an undiluted reminder of your unique services when they eventually compare you to others. If your meeting is 100% verbal, it is inevitable some of your content will get forgotten or weakly relayed.

THE SEVENTH HABIT

Date Your Couple

To find your clients inner most fears, desires and aspirations for their big day, the most personal way to discovery is to meet, befriend and gently question them, watching and feeling for their responses. By 'dating' your prospects you'll experience a two-way level of communication, leading to a deeper relationship that is impossible to replicate by phone or email. If for you 'To meet or not to meet' is still a dilemma, let me be clear that there is no right or wrong answer, you need to do what is right for you. However I will give you my opinion based on experience and results in the hope that if you do not currently 'date' your prospects before quoting you will give it a try. I would say though that the higher you go in price from the average for your industry, the more you should want to meet to explain your value personally:

- *In the past, whenever I have given just a price via telephone or email, 2 out of 10 prospects go onto book; the 8 that do not, raise price objections.*

- *Whenever I meet then quote, 8 out of 10 couple's go onto book, the 2 that do not, raise price objections.*

When I quote via phone or email more often than not I am communicating with price shoppers; when I meet face-to-face, or face to video camera, I am presenting to value buyers.

This is why I am loathed to quote outside of a meeting. Price shoppers are not my avatar and I am prepared to let them go. To deter price shoppers from making premature evaluations based on price, I now include the following passage in my initial enquiry response to keep prospects inside my funnel, not out of it:

"...Because I do things very differently to 99% of my competitors operating in the UK, I can only give prices about your wedding on <event_date_long> at <event_location> after a friendly face-to-face or Skype meeting with you. Why? Well, the unique set of differences I will bring to your wedding cannot be compared to others on price alone..."

Setting the stage

My marketing and sales process is very carefully choreographed, and nothing is left to chance. There are certain things I want my prospects to know about me before we meet to precondition them and raise their expectations that I can over-deliver on their idea of perfection.

1. *I make it clear at the earliest opportunity that a meeting is required before price revelation. Yes this will frustrate and deter price shoppers which is perfect for me because as mentioned above, they are not my avatar. Meetings that convey added value, followed by price increases conversion rates dramatically because the more time a client invests conversing with me or you, the more likely they are to book.*

2. *I have worked very hard to create positive advantages, those unique differences that make me stand out and attract clients. I want my prospects to know what they are in advance of meeting me because I know they will pre-sell couple's and surround me in wedding expert glow before I even say a word.*

3. *I value my time highly and so wherever possible I architect conversations that lead to my prospects travelling to me for the meeting.*

Client Meetings – Where should they take place?

There are a number of meeting options open to wedding creatives, and it is possible you may have used some or all of the following at some point:

Your home/place of work

Assuming of course you have an ideal space and enjoy welcoming brides and grooms into your home/place of work, this is perfect because it allows you to absolutely control the environment in a way that is not possible through any of the other options below. For example, you may have discovered prior to your meeting that your bride and groom love certain genres of music, which you can softly play in the background throughout your meeting providing an atmosphere they will warm to. You can leave letters of testimony on your coffee table and invite prospects to browse through them whilst you excuse yourself to collect refreshments. Should you have accolades or samples these can be left in view. These silent influencers will help get your couple warmed up before you even get into your presentation, and then of course after you've opened your meeting to discover what your couple really want, you can project their personalised presentation on your wall mounted TV for a larger than average experience. No interruptions from guests floating around the venue or hunting for a free sofa to conduct your meeting at a coffee shop. But the biggest benefit comes from the time and effort your couple will have to invest in travelling to you. The more known you are in the wedding industry, and the brighter your expert glow, the more willing couples will be to make the trip out to you, and these prospects can be viewed as highly motivated and having already partially bought into your products or services.

Home/place of work visits also increase your efficiency and productivity as the time it would have taken you for the return trip can now be used for back to back prospect meetings or other Thrive - Zone 1 activities.

Who is this strategy for?

The very busy wedding professional wanting to maximise on time, increase productivity and control the meeting environment. Someone who views home/place of work visits as a measure of pre-commitment on the bride and groom's side.

Home/place of work meetings are my preferred choice.

Their home

What could be more convenient for your bride and groom other than to host the meeting in a comfortable space they are both super relaxed in? And with no effort of travel involved for them this option really is ideal, especially if they have young children. In this instance it is all about the convenience of your couple, and if you have a little time on your hands and do not mind the travel and the expenses incurred, you will be viewed as being very accommodating winning you brownie points.

Who is this strategy for?

The wedding professional who is keen to make the meeting process as convenient as possible for their couple with a little time on their hands and likes business travel.

A coffee shop or something similar

In this instance a mutually convenient meeting spot is chosen, often when there is a considerable distance between both parties which if not used would put the onus of a very long journey on either your avatar or you.

Who is this strategy for?

The wedding professional who views distant prospects as potentially ideal clients so offers this as a halfway house.

The venue

Having chosen their ideal spot, couples can be quite proud of their choice and want to show it off as well as want to re-visit it from time to time for planning purposes, creating a situation for your avatar where they can kill two birds with one stone. Venue meetings provide an opportunity for you to shine especially if you make creative suggestions as prospects walk you through their spaces. This also allows you to really help your couple visualise their day as you walk around the venue and mention what will happen where (pointing at different areas). The more brilliant your ideas are the more they will view you as the expert and begin to build trust in you. It's also a wonderful opportunity to get to know the event manager(s), as a side benefit, remember to take your wedding brochures along with you in case you hit it off with staff and they ask for your details.

Who is this strategy for?

The wedding professional who is keen to meet prospects on-site to see the potential space, and views it as an opportunity to connect with venue management with the possibility of winning additional business there.

Video conference calls

Now and again you may attract the attention of a couple where the distance between the two of you is just too great because they are either in a remote part of your country or in another country altogether. Hosting the meeting on Skype or something similar is perfect in these instances. Did you know its possible to screen share via a Skype call and to easily send files relating to your presentation to your prospects? Used correctly video conference calls can be the next best thing to a face-to-face, you can win valuable business this way.

Who is this strategy for?

The wedding professional who wants to do destination weddings, serve international clients coming 'home' for their wedding or provide a service to distant clients.

There is no right or wrong meeting place, just a preferred location that is right for you and your prospect.

Before we delve into the actual Keynote (or Powerpoint) presentation, 2 things: firstly, if you are weak in any of the 7 influencers detailed in the previous Habit, make it your priority to strengthen them first. The more powerful your influencers, the more influential you will be at meetings. Secondly, don't just copy the presentation word for word, rather use it as a guide to create a unique communication congruent with your USPs, otherwise it simply will not work.

Pre-presentation

Always begin by asking questions about your prospects and their day.

Once you've asked a question stop talking and emphatically listen to your couple's answers, never interrupt their flow other than to ask supplemental questions once their response has come to a natural ending. Let your couple do most of the talking, remember, brides and grooms love pre-living their wedding day so this is the best way to get them to open up and get really excited about the biggest celebration of their lives. Your goal is to get them to reveal precisely what they want and don't want so you can feed it back to them and be what they want you to be when you eventually present.

My favourite opening question is: *"So what's the Love Story between <bride and groom's name>?"*

This will get you impulsive laughs or at a minimum wide smiles offering the perfect way to open the discovery stage of your meeting. When people laugh they relax, when people relax you increase the chances of them liking you and when people like you they are more likely to book you.

It is very important to understand there is a syntax to the meeting order which if juggled will produce different results. It maybe that the reason you are not currently getting the results you want is you could be doing all the right things but in the wrong order, or missing out a step. Let me give you an example of a syntax to help you understand this concept more clearly:

'Johnny ate the fish.' 'The fish ate Johnny.' Identical words, different syntax, very different outcomes for Johnny!

In another example, avoid giving 'upside down prices'. Price revelation should occur after you've articulated value, never before.

My presentation follows a very specific, carefully choreographed syntax and it is important to define a beginning, middle and end. Above all, do everything in your power to make this process a highly personalised experience for your couple for example use their names, wedding date and venue when appropriate during your discussions.

Syntax overview

Beginning

1. *Nobody will give you their total attention unless you surround yourself in an expert glow. Some wedding creatives shy away from this saying they do not want to talk in glowing terms about themselves. To this I say get over it, if you don't who will? Remember you have to think like a bride, and she is thinking she wants the best which is why highlighting your outstanding credentials are key. Prospects will never buy into you if they are unimpressed with your first impression. You must have in mind what attention grabbing benefits you want your avatar to know about you. At this stage you want to instil confidence in your ability to over-deliver. Pre-selling is a prerequisite.*

2. *Set out your positive advantages to consolidate the above.*

3. *Give free gifts to help your avatar blueprint their wedding and steer them into viewing you as their expert based on the quality, value and usefulness of the free information you openly give. Brides are thinking they want the overwhelm and stress to go away and are looking for a 'done for you solution' so they can relax and enjoy their day. Aim to be that 'done for you' person. Design your wedding experience to de-stress and delight.*

4. *Unless you offer a venue, let prospects know that many venue's*

list you as a preferred supplier. Why? To trigger the power of social proof. Having high numbers of luxurious wedding venue's endorse you via a listing as a preferred supplier adds credibility to your positioning as the go-to person in your industry. If you are not yet listed in high numbers, keep getting better at your craft until venue's notice you. If you soar above the average supplier in your field and are different enough it is a matter of time before your invitation to be listed comes.

Middle

5. *Now is the time to deliver your message, never before. Having set the stage as the expert capable of over-delivering, your avatar will be open and receptive to your message. Aim to solidify a true and certain belief at a deeply emotional level that you can meet all expectations. Do this successfully and your couple will decide you are the one for them, before you even get to price; more often than not.*

End

6. *Always read out an emphatic testimonial before price revelation to put prospects in an emotional state because remember, hiring a wedding supplier is an emotional not a rational decision. Your bride and groom will use logic afterwards to justify the price.*

7. *Declare prices – If you have resonated with your couple, by now they will be ready to buy and you'll have no need to sell. It will not be about price, rather which prescription will be right for them.*

The better your ability to articulate value and convey worth, the easier you will find it to book your avatar.

OK, having talked about the presentation, let's see it in action...

THE EIGHTH HABIT

Present In A Way That Prescribes Not Sells

Message to convey:

Personalisation makes your bride and groom feel special. USPs begin to build trust and create your expert glow. If you do not have any USPs yet, be proactive and take action today so you have something to differentiate you from your competition tomorrow, because couples will always pay more for differences than they will for similarities. Brides and grooms will also pay more for who you are, rather than what you do so make a name for yourself. Think what positive advantage you can use to magnetise higher paying couple's to you.

Influencers incorporated:

1, 3, 4, 5, 6

Floor-Filling

Message to convey:

Show off what you do best, never lose sight of your core business, illustrate the added value that your expertise can bring to your avatar's day.

Influencers incorporated:

3 and 4.

Hannah & Shaun, You...

wish your wedding entertainment to be special and unique.

are in love, and want a packed dance floor where everyone has fun.

would like wedding entertainment that is filled with love and laughter.

are passionate about the way in which your entertainment unfolds.

I...

love people, weddings, music and entertaining.

will put my heart and soul into the biggest day of your life.

will create unique and emotive moments, beyond fantastic, floor filling music.

am passionate about reflecting your idea of the perfect wedding.

Message to convey:

People hire people they like, trust and have huge amounts of confidence in. Empathise with their wants, let them know you understand what they need, show you have a passion and desire to over deliver on their idea of perfection and watch them warm to you.

Influencers incorporated:

1,3 and 4.

Personalised guarantee
for when you say "I Do"

I promise you'll love everything
"I do" or your money back...

...& with a 100% satisfaction
record, you can be certain your
day will flow exactly as you wish.

Message to convey:

Shock and grab attention. Pattern interupt. Eliminate risk. Move prospects further down your sales funnel.

It's unlikely that many others in your category will offer a money-back guarantee, which will instantly elevate you above your crowded market. It underpins your inner confidence and drive to passionately over-deliver.

Influencers incorporated:

1,3 and 4.

Message to convey:

Reiterate your positive advantage in a different way. You want to make it impossible for your couple to think you are like any other supplier they will see. What can you do to present yourself as the 'Usain Bolt' in your industry? Remember if you have nothing today, consistently take action until you have a differentiator tomorrow because if there is nothing unique about you, you leave yourself open to being commoditised and price shopped. Achieving accolades is one way to get brides hunting for you, but by no means the only way. Think creatively, how will you standout?

Influencers incorporated:

1, 3 ,4, 6 and 7.

I am a preferred DJ at nearly **50** luxury venues inc…

Message to convey:

Venue endorsements are powerful influencers. Let it be known that venues cherry-pick the very best suppliers, and many point to you. Professional endorsements are very persuasive because now the industry is saying you are amazing, as opposed to you. If you cannot demonstrate this yet, work harder until you become listed at venues. It can be done and you have the capabilities to do it. The secret to getting listed is to excel in your field of expertise. Step up, keep raising your bar until venues start inviting you to be listed.

Influencers incorporated:

1, 3 ,4, 6 and 7.

6x Award Winner Inc.
Best Wedding DJ in England

Over 100 couples that I've entertained were asked to rate my services
as part of the TWIA awards judging process. This is what they think of me:

Voter Question	2013 Ave Score	2014 Ave Score	2015 Ave Score
Range of options (eg: sound, lighting, music styles) made available by your DJ	9.5	10.0	9.9
Quality of expertise, advice and guidance received from your DJ	9.7	10.0	9.9
Quality of customer service and communications received from your DJ	9.5	9.9	9.8
Your DJ's punctuality and personal presentation on the day of your wedding	10.0	10.0	10.0
The level at which your DJ delivered what was booked	9.8	10.0	10.0
Quality of your DJ's web presence (web site, Facebook etc)	9.6	9.9	9.6
Value for money	9.3	9.8	9.8
Overall average score	9.6	9.9	9.9

Message to convey:

Endorsements from previous couple's add credibility at a level you cannot reach yourself no matter how well you articulate it. Increase faith in your data by using a third party to carry out your survey. Learn to think like a bride. When your avatar faces uncertain choices, more often than not she will look to see what others did to get pleasurable outcomes and will quite often follow.

Influencers incorporated:

1, 3 ,4, 6 and 7.

Let me help plan
the most exciting
day of your life

I live and breathe creative weddings and have performed at over 700 celebrations.

Revealing some of the expert knowledge gained through my experiences, is one of the greatest free gifts I can give you.

I know you are trying to figure out how to get married via the internet, or through friends and family. I know the answers to most of your entertainment questions and want to help, simply because I can.

Trust me to guide you through your wedding day options, and I'll spark ideas within you, setting your creative mind racing.

By the end, you will be well on your way to forming a crystal clear blueprint for the happiest day of your life.

Message to convey:

Let you avatar know this is not your first rodeo. She definitely wants to know you are an expert she can trust and lean on for the perfect day.

It's important to note that you are yet to present your services. What you have done up to this stage in your presentation is to create your expert glow. Always do this before explaining your products or services, because your expert glow goes a long way to pre-selling your avatar and building anticipation, excitement and high expectations.

Influencers incorporated:

1, 3, 4, 6 and 7.

CHAPTER 1: Prelude
Hannah & Shaun, ignite emotion from the moment guests arrive with 30 minutes of romantic background music

CHAPTER 2: Procession
Your favourite ballad will play as you walk up the aisle to marry the love of your life

CHAPTER 3: Signatures
Select 4 love songs as you sign the register and pose for photos

CHAPTER 4: Recession
Then float back down the aisle to your celebration track as guests cheer and applaud you as the new Mr & Mrs Robinson!

You'll need romantic music for your wedding in four chapters

Message to convey:

Now that you've laid the foundation of your expert status, your avatar will be more open to listening attentively to your message, in fact by now your couple may even have decided they want you. Anticipation and high expectation are key. As you move into the next phase, begin by offering free expert guidance. Your bride has an overall picture to paint. Think how you can help put the pieces of the wedding jigsaw together making it easier for her.

Influencers incorporated:

1, 2, 3 and 4.

Lets look at your Timeline at
Offely Place

Start Time	End Time	Activity
1.00pm	1.30pm	Guests arrive at Offely Place
1.30pm	2.00pm	You'll get married!
2.00pm	3.30pm	Canapés, drinks and photos
3.30pm	3.40pm	Room inspection & photos of couple in room
3.40pm	4.00pm	Receiving line
4.00pm	4.05pm	Grand Entrance
4.05pm	5.30pm	Wedding breakfast
5.30pm	6.00pm	Speeches
6.00pm	8.00pm	Evening guests arrive & Reception begins
8.00pm	8.10pm	Cake cut
8.15pm	8.20pm	1st Dance
8.20pm	8.25pm	Father / bride (if having)
8.30pm	10.30pm	Evening buffet
11.55pm	12.00am	Tunnel of Love or Circle of Love to close
12.00am		Carriages

Message to convey:

Another way to give free help is to provide a personalised timeline. All couples need one. Outline the various chapters of your avatar's day based on the start time for their wedding. Your potential bride and groom will be very thankful for the heads-up, especially if their venue has not yet provided an overview - but more importantly guess who they now view as their knowledgable and trusted expert? Take a moment to choose what free valuable advice you could give away to make prospects feel more confident and excited about hiring you to ensure the right outcome for their day.

Influencers incorporated:

1, 2, 3 and 4.

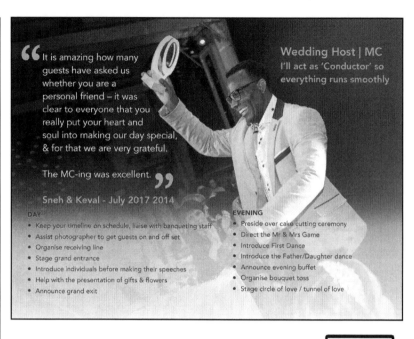

Message to convey:

Communicate your main wedding experience and up sells in positive, professional and powerfully magnetic ways bringing in emphatic testimonials here and there. Social proof builds trust, and trust is a vital ingredient in getting booked.

Influencers incorporated:

1,3 and 4.

To throw, or not to throw? That is the question

- Throw it
- Throw a replica
- Display it at home
- Have it pressed and framed
- Throw one of the bridesmaids flowers
- Give it to an elder family member who has influenced your life, it may mean so much more to them than if a girlfriend of your age catches it
- Take it to the final resting place of someone close to you who is no longer with us

Message to convey:

Another gem your bride will love centres around the bouquet. Most brides only ever consider 'throwing' or 'keeping' their bouquet but there are other options, some quite touching, and when you present an idea couple's emotionally connect to, you create a powerful moment when your expert glow brightens, and your couple draw closer to you.

Another killer tip most photographers probably know: When cake cutting have the groom on the left hand side with his right arm around his brides waist. The bride holds a knife in her right hand, cupping her left hand on top, exposing her wedding ring. The groom's left hand rests on top of his brides hand; now when they push down to cut the cake, both wedding rings, are clearly visible in each shot. What other a-ha ideas would your couple treasure?

Influencers incorporated:

1, 2, 3 and 4.

Add additional slides to emotionally convey your wedding experience in glowing terms

Message to convey:

Having positioned yourself as the trusted expert, go ahead and wow them as to how and why your signature wedding experience would best serve your couple.

The key to the success of your presentation deck is to weave in as many of the influencers as you can. Your number one goal is to think like a bride, and her thoughts are, she wants the best so powerfully persuade her that you are what she wants you to be.

Red Flag

If you are not yet able to make use of all the influencers because of gaps in your skill set, make it a high priority to attain them because they provide the fastest and most direct route to turning you into a client magnet.

> Dear Terry,
> Well, it's a month now since our special day. Paul and I are back from our honeymoon and slowly catching up on things. Hard to get back to work and laundry after being a princess for two weeks. But the feeling of love and the amazing memories still float through our days and in our hearts. Hard to express how beautiful and deeply meaningful our wedding was to us both. The love and joy seemed to just swirl around us all...
>
> ... and so much of that was because of you!
>
> Terry, we are so grateful that we found you. Your presence, smile, professionalism, steady calm, guidance, not to mention your first class MC talents just made our day everything it was. We knew when we met you that we'd be in the very best of hands and indeed we were. Because of you, we could relax, and enjoy and just 'be' present and in the precious moments, and for that we will be forever thankful. You are a star and we hope a new friend.
> Sending love and thanks,
> Barbara and Paul

Message to convey:

Emotion.

A wedding is one of most emotional lifetime purchases your avatar will ever make with the heart often over ruling the head on budget.

Testimonial before price

Always put your couple into an emotional state before price revelation by quoting an emphatic testimonial that poignantly points to how your avatar will feel after using you. Getting other people to rave about you is a very powerful way to achieve this because they can talk about you in a way you cannot.

Influencers incorporated:

1,3 and 4.

Benefit Driven Solutions		
Your highest valued solution ££££	**Your middle valued solution** £££	**Your lowest valued solution** ££
• Benefit driven solution	• Benefit driven solution	• Benefit driven solution
• Benefit driven solution	• Benefit driven solution	• Benefit driven solution
• Benefit driven solution	• Benefit driven solution	• Benefit driven solution
• Benefit driven solution	• Benefit driven solution	
• Benefit driven solution	• Benefit driven solution	
• Benefit driven solution	• Benefit driven solution	
• Benefit driven solution		
• Benefit driven solution		
• Benefit driven solution		
• Benefit driven solution		
• Benefit driven solution		
• Benefit driven solution		

Message to convey:

Price revelation: If you powerfully show up for yourself during your presentation and irresistibly become what your prospect deeply desire, brides and grooms will have made up their minds that they want you way before you get to price.

Your goal is to leave prospects feeling excited and that nothing on earth could be better than what you and only you can provide. Get your avatar fizzing with excitement through honest and truthful marketing and their wish to have you will far outweigh the above average price you charge. This is how you relegate price off the top spot of the decision making process.

Remember, getting premium buyers to pursue you is easy once you've mastered how to prescribe, not sell.

Earlier I asked *'To meet or not to meet, that is the question?'*

Can you see now why 8 out of 10 book me after a face-to-face or Skype presentation and why only 2 out of 10 book me when given a price without having created the opportunity to explain the added value? This is because the more you charge the greater the need to convey value in order to diminish the importance of price, present yourself as excellent value for money, then ultimately move yourself into the arena of the 'must have' wedding supplier. Master the art of transitioning prospects through these phases and you will position yourself beyond competition.

Recap

You are about 2/3rds through this guide to magnifying your wedding business by attracting higher paying brides so let's take a moment to reflect on how far you have come. You've discovered:

- *It's much easier marketing to an avatar than trying to be all things to all brides.*

- *The benefits of positioning, packaging, promoting and partnering to couple's with higher budgets.*

- *What you need to do right now to hit your 3 year income, lifestyle and freedom goals.*

- *The importance of apportioning at least 51% of your time daily to Thrive - Zone 1 activities.*

- *7 powerful influencers to magnetise higher paying clients to you.*

- *Why you should always convey value before giving a price*

- *Effective presentation skills that prescribe not sell.*

Success loves speed. Do not waste a second of the 86,400 you have been gifted with today. Procrastination will only delay your success. Take immediate action in applying these strategies and transform your business into the company it was designed to be.

At this point you'll be thinking 1 of 2 things:

1. *"I've got the intel I need and the reigns in my hands...I'm off to the races with the Habits I've learnt so far!."*

Or

2. *"I'm going to need a little support incorporating the Habits into the fabric of my business practises." In which case my 1-1 Mentoring Program, or online course will be perfect for you; discover more at: www.weddingmarketingmastery.co.uk*

THE NINTH HABIT

Climb To The Pinnacle Of The Pyramid

Be unique.

Be passionate.

Be the best.

There is no place for silver or bronze medal holders at the top. In our new world, the politically correct stance is to say it's the taking part that counts not the winning.

By reading The 12 Habits I know this stance is not for you. To gain the favour of venues you need to be better than the other suppliers they see in your field of expertise in order to become preferred. They can pick from literally hundreds of suppliers who do what you do... hundreds. And those who set their sights on being in the middle of the pack rarely get listed. I'm here to tell you that venue managers wear many hats on the day of a wedding, they ensure the chef is on time with the meal, the venue looks stunning, the bride and groom are well looked after, they oversee the photographer, videographer, florist, entertainment and all other wedding creatives hired by the bride and groom on the day. They are also talent scouts and will seek you out for an invitation, but only if your signature wedding experience moves people emotionally and is beyond compare to the feeling created by other suppliers in your line of expertise. To be chosen to represent a venue, you have to excel, be outstanding, rise above what is expected of someone in your profession. The best way to explain it is really through the real life experience of a couple on their wedding day. What follows is a touching thank you note to a wedding supplier that I found online. I've removed the creatives name and profession because it is not about that individual, it's about how that wedding professional made the bride and groom feel. I replaced the creatives name with <your name>, and whenever you see this, I want you to say your name out loud because I want you to imagine this letter was written to you:

Hi <your name>,

I've been putting off writing this email for a while, because I don't quite know how to put into words our gratitude for all you did for us in the lead up to our big day and on the day itself.

Quite simply, we don't think our wedding would have been quite the same without you! You went above and beyond the call of duty and we wouldn't hesitate to recommend you to anyone for your <specific wedding> services.

As you know, I in particular was very stressed leading up to the wedding due to problems we were having with our venue with communication and with the timeline for the day.

<Your name> you took the time to speak to us on numerous occasions to find out exactly what we wanted for our day, guiding us with your wealth of knowledge and experience. You then stepped in and communicated with the venue directly, so that the stress was completely taken out of my hands. After knowing that you were dealing with the situation, I felt completely at ease and it made such a difference having that weight off my mind when there was so much else to deal with in those last few weeks.

On the day itself, you arrived early and came to see me and I genuinely felt that you were as excited as us to be sharing in the occasion.

Throughout the day you were on hand for anything we needed or any questions we had. You spoke to the guests and made them feel welcome, you co-ordinated everyone for pictures and ensured that we had all of the group shots we wanted, you communicated with our bridesmaids and ushers wherever necessary and generally did anything that was needed so that our day ran smoothly. … Throughout the day so many of our guests commented on how fantastic you were, from the day guests who you co-ordinated and managed in an entertaining way, to the evening guests who you greeted at the door and welcomed to our reception. Everyone kept asking 'who is <your name>', and were shocked to be told '<your name> is our … <state your profession>'!

You did all of this with a huge smile on your face. In fact, I can't remember a single time during the whole day seeing you without a smile on your face. Your passion for the job is clear for everyone to see.

You were a negotiator, an organiser, and a host and we can't thank you enough for all you did for us.

Mr and Mrs Scott xxx

Here's what I know about the secret to getting listed at 4 and 5 star wedding venues: It begins with you being honest. Look at the last batch of thank you's that you received from your clients. If they are generic, short and polite it means you are doing a good job that was appreciated, but therein lies the problem! It means you are OK, maybe slightly above average, but there is headroom for you to become outstanding and you must fill that gap. Your mark of outstanding excellence will be identified to you when you receive letters like the one above, relevant to your own field of expertise. I'm here to tell you that when your bride and groom float out of their wedding venue feeling like nothing on earth could have gone better, because of the part you played on the biggest day of their life, that will be the day venue managers begin to ask you to become a preferred supplier; the two go hand in hand. Being OK, or slightly above average rarely triggers an invitation to become a preferred supplier, to become listed you have to be beyond compare.

When your couple push aside the generic thank you's they send to every other supplier, and write you deeply a personalised, heartfelt message because of the way you served them, venue managers will have already noticed the magic you created long before your couple's letter lands on your doormat, or pings into your inbox. Create deep emotions for your bride and groom and venue managers will feel compelled to choose you as a preferred supplier and this is how you will create a pipeline of qualified leads from luxury venues direct to your inbox for yourself.

In my humble opinion getting listed by premium venue's in this way is the single most effective Thrive - Zone 1 activity you can undertake, because by climbing and remaining at the highest level, and becoming noticed and known for what you do, you'll be pursued by brides and grooms for as long as you are in business, but the real beauty is couple's will be seeking you out by email whilst you sleep, holiday, party or work. This is wedding marketing at its best and is known as passive marketing. Step up to the passive marketing level and you will never be out of work.

Other ways to get listed

I said there was only one truly effective way to get on the preferred list of luxury venue's and I believe the way described above to be it, however there are other routes to being listed, but the probability of them working is much lower:

Cold call and meet

At the time of writing, Google is the most powerful search engine in the world, type in a relevant search term such as 'Luxury wedding venues in <your town>' and the results will be displayed on your screen in seconds. Shortlist the venue's you want to work at, call asking who the wedding and event manager is, speak to them directly (not a colleague) introducing your company, highlighting your differences. If you are similar to the other creatives in your industry, without genuine USPs you will struggle to get a foot in the door, so be proactive and make it your priority to create USPs first. Don't try to get listed via telephone, post, email or by just sending them to your site as you will drastically reduce your chances of success, in fact this is practically a waste of time. The event manager may pay you lip service but unless you are well known and your reputation for excellence precedes you, I can't imagine a reputable venue recommending anyone to their high paying brides without having seen their work first, can you? It would be like trying to get a job without a face-to-face interview. You must first impress to get venues to express an interest in listing you.

Verdict: I've tried the 'Cold call and meet' strategy and it is somewhat possible but will eat up a lot of your valuable Thrive - Zone 1 time, and has a very low success rate.

Being in the right place at the right time

Wedding supplier placements can last for years but they never last forever. At some point the listed creative will move on either by choice or otherwise, creating an opportunity. If you are well known in your industry for being an outstanding wedding creative you will be high on the venue's wanted list. I know of a wedding creative who was approached under similar circumstances, who because of who he was rather than for what he did was able to negotiate rates nearly 3 times that of the outgoing wedding supplier.

Venue managers also (inconveniently) move on, and their departure can also lead to your departure especially if the new manager has license to bring in a team from the outside resulting in your pipeline of referrals grinding to a halt... An unsavoury situation I found myself in a few years ago: Maria Scullion was an event manager I got on well with at Dartmouth House in Mayfair, London. After a while I noticed

I'd not been receiving enquiries from brides and grooms marrying there. I later discovered that Maria had moved on, a new manger had been appointed and hand-picked a new list of wedding creatives she already had a relationship with and I was out! I learnt a very harsh lesson... a lesson I never forgot.

I thought *"how can I guard against this ever happening to me again?"* and reminisced on my City days and how my bosses discovered the hobbies, interests and passions of their top clients then matched them with tickets to Wimbledon, cricket, football, rugby, opera, theatre, the races etc. I could not compete with a corporate entertainment budget like that but I could engage in corporate entertainment on a much smaller scale. So when I got listed at the fabulous St. James' hotel around the corner from Buckingham Palace, I discovered that the venue manager, Rochelle Payne loved the former chart topping group JLS, so when I heard they were holding a farewell concert at the London o2 Arena I got her a ticket. The effect to my referrals was incredible, and when she eventually left the luxury wedding venue, guess what happened? She personally called me to say she was moving on. She invited me in for a handover meeting with her incoming replacement, at the same time I was introduced to two other new members in the event team. During the meeting she announced "...This is Terry, he is our preferred supplier, please send any enquires to him..." at the time of writing I get on very well with the new event manager and my pipeline of enquiries flows without interruption. How different to my Dartmouth House experience! The moral of the story is when something negative happens to you in your business or personal life, analyse what caused it, create a solution to guard against it from ever happening again and implement your solution by taking immediate action, remember never let procrastination prevent you from achieving your dream.

Put down roots

You will have to work very hard to get listed at your top venues, so don't let them slip through your hands once you become chosen. Learn from my mistake, get to know your event managers on a personal as well as a business level if you want to protect what you have. Don't just send them a Christmas card each December most suppliers do that and you'll simply get lost amongst the other cards on your contacts desk, only to have your card cleared off and binned early January. Make touches that he or she will really value throughout the year, if you value your opportunities.

Verdict: Being in the right place at the right time is not about luck; it's about staying ready not getting ready so when opportunity presents itself to you are in the perfect position to capitalise on it.

New builds

Keep an eye out for new builds going up in the areas you want to work in. Then make a point of reaching out to the person responsible for weddings and events before the paint goes on the walls. Ask for the meeting and let them know your USPs, but don't just go in with your want to be listed. Think what do they need? Their goal is to secure bookings, so think like the event team would. Help them achieve their goals. Their number one priority will be to get new bookings, and you could let your couples know about the new venue if they are still searching for a stage to host their wedding on. If you offered to promote the new build to your tribe via blogs, site listings, Facebook, Twitter and other social media platforms, do you think you could trigger the law of reciprocity? Is it likely the new venue would be more inclined to list you?

Verdict: A good strategy that works well especially if you have a good reputation in the industry and a large social media following.

Pay for advertising space

Some luxury venues do not have a preferred list, instead they charge advertising space on their websites, brochures and magazines and promote you to couples that way. Look out for busy luxurious wedding venues that offer this as it is a superb way to get listed, in fact this offers a brilliant route to a brides attention, because by paying to appear in a venue's literature you create an impression that you have the venue's endorsement and for some couple's third party recommendations help govern their buying decisions. This strategy is most effective at venue's that run 70+ weddings each year which is the minimum number you should be looking for when selecting which wedding venue's to spend your advertising budget with.

Verdict: This is a targeted way to place your company directly in front of your ideal client, but the key to maximising results is in knowing which venues to advertise with. Test and measure adverts, your rule should be if you win business from it that dwarfs the cost of advertising then keep on doing it, but if your advert fails to bring in enquiries stop it on expiry. Don't think it will turn around, it won't.

6 Reasons your advert may fail

1. *Headline does not speak to your avatar*

2. *Uninspiring copy*

3. *Poor quality or irrelevant image*

4. *Advert is placed online or in a publication that has a low readership*

5. *Promotion may have erroneous contact details*

6. *It could be as simple as the wrong colours being used*

Good wedding copy achieves 3 goals

1. *Grabs the attention of your bride and groom*

2. *Arouses enthusiasm and interest in your wedding experience*

3. *Compels your avatar to take the desired next step which is usually to reach out and contact you.*

Become a wordsmith and master the art of persuasive copywriting or if it's not your forte, hire someone to do it for you. Either way you have to communicate your message with such power that it demands the response you desire. This is an essential requirement if you are to succeed in your endeavour to book higher paying brides.

THE TENTH HABIT

Stop Dragging Buckets And Install Pipelines

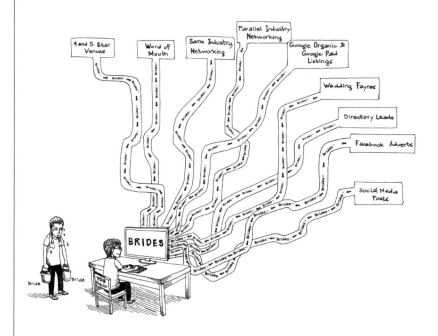

When I started out as a wedding supplier I worked very, very hard and rarely smart, I hunted brides instead of setting myself up to be hunted by them. I slogged daily by manually trawling through the data spreadsheets I purchased from wedding directories or blindly fished around hoping to muster up new prospects from any source possible. It was a crazy, scattered strategy and to be honest, I did not know any better. Nobody was showing me how to pick the low hanging fruit. I thought as long as I was working long hours I would breakthrough, truth is I was treading water, nothing changed. I was dragging buckets instead of installing pipelines. If you can relate to this, there is a better way.

It begins and ends with the actions you take.

Throughout The 12 Habits I've reiterated the necessity for you to create a positive advantage in a similar way that Apple have in the computer world. Get excellent at what you do. Be unique, passionate and always over-deliver. Get to this level and you will create an army of raving fans that will drive brides into your pipeline for you. Your goal is to create as many pipelines as possible capable of doing a lot of your marketing for you...passively.

There are many, marketing strategies for you to choose from, the secret is in knowing which strategies to use, and more importantly how to prioritise them so you allocate proportionate amounts of Thrive - Zone 1 time cultivating them. What follows is the order in which I prioritise my own marketing pyramid based on the effectiveness of my own real life success stories. Customise the lower half of your pyramid to suit your business, but I highly recommend not tinkering with the order of the top four. The top four represent your passive marketing pipeline, which is without question the most powerful form of lead-generating tools you can employ to work for you and therefore demands your attention.

 Marketing Pyramid Segment 1:

Your 'Golden Triangle'

At the top of your Marketing Pyramid is your 'Golden Triangle'. The passive marketing asset capable of feeding your pipeline with your most lucrative source of higher paying prospects. Do the work correctly once and get pre-qualified leads forever. It is for this reason you should spend most of your Zone 1 time working your Golden Triangle. Begin by getting brilliant at what you do to ease your way in to an abundance of luxury venue's - remember top wedding locations will only cherry-pick the best, so be that go-to brand. Notice I encourage you to attract an abundance of luxury venues, and there are 2 reasons for this:

1. *Should you ever find yourself in the 'Dartmouth House' situation I found myself in several years ago, you'll hit the deck running taking comfort in the fact that you have a plethora of other luxury*

venue's pipelining avatar's to you, allowing you time to find a replacement for the one you lost, whilst remaining free from financial panic. In other words, by carrying out this protective and valuable Thrive - Zone 1 activity today, you will potentially keep yourself out of financial difficulties at some time in the future.

2. *It provides you with a surplus of potential bookings, which you will need for the networking segment of your pyramid, I'll cover this in a few paragraphs.*

Marketing Pyramid Segment 2:

 Word of mouth from your brides, grooms and guests

Whenever you serve brides and grooms on their wedding day aim to exceed their expectations, in so doing you'll create an army of raving fans that will shout your brilliance from the roof tops to the extent that whenever they plan a wedding or event in the future you'll become their number 1 choice.

Being good or OK at what you do is no longer good enough, and certainly not a target for you. Why? Well, when creatives provide a service in the good or OK zone, potential wedding planners will think someone else could be better simply because you did not set yourself apart from the other suppliers in your category. Excel, be outstanding, and in peak wedding season (and from time to time around the edges) your supply will be outstripped by demand. Operate in the average zone and the reverse will be true.

Marketing Pyramid Segment 3:

 Word of mouth from a same industry network referral group

Hand-pick 4 other wedding suppliers operating in the same industry as yourself to join your networking group; for example if you are a wedding photographer invite 4 other togs to refer work to. To get the most out of this marketing strategy follow these simple guidelines:

- *Only invite professionals operating at a similar level to your own, not below. This way you can be certain your referrals will not disappoint.*

- *Pick same industry professionals that target higher paying couples as well. Why? If their marketing strategy is to target brides looking for bargains and you market to couples at the other end of the spectrum, your referrals will clash resulting in both of you experiencing the frustrations of pitching to a mis-matched prospect.*

- *Limit your same industry referral group to 4 plus you, so 5 in total. This may seem odd advice and you may think the more the merrier, but in my humble opinion 4 plus you is the optimum number for a networking referral group. Why? Invite more and too few will get work, invite less and the benefit is diluted.*

- *Ensure all members do a similar number of weddings, for example if you average 60 weddings a year it's important the others do as well to ensure you are all giving and taking at a fairly even rate. It means you are all likely to generate a similar number of surplus enquiries which you can refer within your group.*

Set this up correctly from the outset and your same industry network referral group will form wings of its own, installing a pipeline of higher paying brides direct to your computer, and the beauty is this passive marketing even happens whilst you engage in Lifestyle – Zone 3 activities.

In closing, this strategy will increase your marketing team by 4 with the added sweetener that you'll do so at virtually no cost to yourself. Failing to implement this strategy is nothing short of making a conscious decision not to make use of an expert marketing department offering to work for you unsalaried.

Marketing Pyramid Segment 4:

Word of mouth from a parallel industry network referral group

In a similar fashion to the same industry network referral group, the parallel industry network referral group requires you to create relationships with wedding creatives in a different none competing field of expertise, so if you are a florist team-up with photographers, room-stylists, singers, chair cover businesses, caterers, any wedding business that is different but complimentary to your own. To get the most out of this strategy, follow the bulleted guidelines you will use for your same industry network referral group. Do this correctly and you'll gain another 4 marketing professionals into your wedding business.

But here's The Juice, by combining the same industry strategy with the parallel industry strategy, you'll ignite a three-fold synergistic effect generating exponential benefits to your wedding business potentially worth hundreds of thousands!

1. *You will increase your marketing team from 1 (assuming there is only you in the company) to 8 plus you at virtually zero cost to yourself.*

2. *Your 'free marketing team' will be highly effective at generating leads, and 'join your company' fully experienced and fully trained.*

3. *According to Payscale.com if you were to employ a Marketing Manger (at the time of writing) it would cost you £32,565 pa. Multiply that by 8, the number of 'employees' you could have in your business and it should cost you £260,520! That's right, £260,520 worth of managerial, fully trained personnel at practically zero cost to you. Granted, your marketing team will not be working for you full time, they will be primarily working on their own businesses, but surely you can see the incredible benefits in installing these pipelines.*

Red Flag

Failing to employ one of these networking strategies is to consciously limit the growth of your business, but to deny your company both is nothing short of crazy.

Marketing Pyramid Segment 5:

Google - Organic listing

Google is the world's favourite search engine, it's where most internet savvy, higher paying brides and grooms go to find the suppliers they need for an amazing wedding. If you cannot be found quickly on Google, you will be leaving money on the table for your competitors to scoop up.

Make it your online goal to organically dominate the first page of Google (and other popular search engines like Yahoo) for the keywords you want to be found for. Do not be discouraged by people who tell you 'It can't be done'. I'm here to tell you that it can and has been done by others, remember, what one man or woman has done another man or woman can do – but it does require consistent action. So let me give you some examples. My dear friend Hollie Kamel set up a wedding singer business and knew the importance of a top ranking. She diligently studied and applied white hat SEO and social media strategies and in just 9 months, went from being nowhere to oscillating through positions 1-3 on the first page of Google for the keyword search terms she wanted to be found for. Never let the words of others fix a false ceiling above your head, constantly breakthrough. If your Google position sucks, hire an expert with a proven track record in search engine optimisation and social media optimisation skills and aim for the top spot. Someone has to occupy it, that person needs to be you.

Let me share with you two personal experiences. Prior to finding my place in the wedding industry, I ran a salsa promotions company called Salsa Chillout and through the long term application of white hat strategies under the guidance of a SEO expert, our company dominated the first page of Google for the search terms we wanted to be found for: 'Salsa in Essex', 'Salsa lessons in Essex', and 'Salsa dance shoes'. In fact the SEO techniques for the dance shoes arm of our company was so effective, we out-ranked the company brands whose shoes we sold!

I also helped to set up Mwah! Catering a caribbean wedding catering company, and got it ranked number 1 for the search term 'Caribbean wedding catering'. The spin-off allowed us to work alongside TV celebrity chef Levi Roots at the Notting Hill Carnival, and to go on to serve a host of household named celebrities.

Do the same for your wedding business, out-rank your competitors, soar above them on Google, dominate your ground and you will get a stream of online enquiries.

Having a brilliant website that adds value, solves the problems of brides and grooms, and ranks highly on Google is a formula you should crave if you want a powerful pipeline of higher paying brides to grow your wedding business.

Google - Paid listing

As you go through the process of optimising your site with intent to dominate the first page of Google, please don't just sit there waiting for the paint to dry, because you will be waiting for months. In the interim, start a Google Ads campaign for instant first page results. By way of a simplistic overview, you will appear in the Google Ads section on page listings for the search terms you want to be found for, and charged accordingly. At the time of writing a paid advert will appear in the top 3 listings above the organic results with the word Ad highlit in yellow to distinguish it from the organic results. The other paid ads will appear down the right hand side of the page and these will also be clearly annotated with the word Ad, high-lit in yellow. It is most likely that your advert will oscillate through the listings so if it's listed in position 5 today it could for example rank number 3 or 9 tomorrow.

This is precisely what I did at a time when one of my websites was organically listed on page 5 or 6 of Google; a ranking that made me practically invisible to my target audience and if you rank organically on a page other than 1 or 2 on Google (and other search engines) don't kid yourself, you are practically invisible as well. Why? Well think about the way you surf the net. You flit from one site to the next hunting for the one that you like and confidently solves your problem. Extensive research suggests that you have just 8 seconds to capture the attention of your surfer before they are gone forever. Internet surfers flick and scan sites and make decisions in seconds, so know this; you are less likely to attract and book higher paying brides if your content repels, or if you are ranked on anything other than page 1 or 2 either organically or paid for. When allocating your marketing budget Google Ads should be high up simply because of the volume of targeted brides and grooms you can be put in front of 24/7.

Failing to employ a high ranking strategy on Google, either organically or paid for, is like choosing to go to war against your competitors with bows and arrows as opposed to using todays latest technologically advanced weaponry. If you are serious about being in business, make it your business to obtain high rankings on Google and Yahoo and create a marketing pipeline that works for you every 86,400 seconds of every day.

Marketing Pyramid Segment 6:

 Wedding fairs

This is a popular topic with many of my one-to-one and online students so I'm going to dive deeper here and provide more content on this subject than I have with the other pipelines.

Let's start by discovering what your beliefs are about wedding fairs. From the choices below please circle the response you most closely relate to:

A. *I've done wedding fairs in the past but they don't work for me so I don't invest in them anymore, they are a complete waste of time and money.*

B. *I want to exhibit at wedding fairs but the ones I've done have been poorly attended by brides. If I knew where the busy ones where, I would definitely hire a stand.*

C. *I rent spaces at wedding fairs and hope to get one or two bookings to cover the cost of my overheads. Any more is a bonus.*

D. *Wedding fairs are an abundant source of higher paying brides. My goal is to book a considerable proportion of the brides who express an interest in me at a wedding fair, not on the day but as part of my follow-up process.*

E. *I have gone full circle, I have an abundance of ideal clients beating a path to my business, I no longer need this strategy.*

No matter how you've responded, I know exactly how you feel because I have circled all 5 answers at various points along my timeline as a wedding creative. Today, without hesitation my answer is E, but if yours is not E (yet) don't worry I can help.

If your response is A:

'I've done wedding fairs in the past but they don't work for me so I don't invest in them anymore, they are a complete waste of time and money.'

Can I ask you to re-open your mind to a new frame of reference? I am here to tell you that there are some excellent wedding fairs offering generous returns on investment. The insider secret is in knowing how to follow a strategic plan for identifying the best ones then extracting the maximum number of leads out of your fair on the day, read on, I've given '7 Steps to Attract & Book Brides at a Wedding Fair' towards the end of this section.

If you circled B:

'I want to exhibit at wedding fairs but the ones I've done have been poorly attended to by brides. If I knew where the busy ones where, I would definitely hire a stand.'

You will be much easier to help because you already know you should attend fairs, your circle of concern is in discovering where the decent ones are. Here's how to seek them out:

- Firstly, there are optimum times of the year when the majority of wedding fairs take place and these are February - April and September - November. Pick fairs that fall in these months because brides are conditioned through magazines and the internet to expect fairs at these times. Savvy organisers know this and gain extra promotional muscle by surfing this wave. Organisers bucking the trend of the wedding fair seasons have more advertising to do as they will need to put in a bigger push to raise awareness. Trend buckers also tend to be newer to the wedding fair circuit and put them on 'off-peak' because 'peak' dates have already been secured by seasoned organisers. Finally they tend to be attended by less busy wedding creatives, why so? Summertime is when most couple's choose to marry, simply because they want good weather for their special day. Popular wedding suppliers will be booked in the heart of the summer months leaving organisers with fewer wedding creatives able to attend even if they wanted to. This can be advantageous to you though, especially if you have recently set-up your wedding business, or operate in an overcrowded market space such as wedding photography. My opinion though is you should attend established fairs operating in the normal cycle.

- Always visit fairs you are considering renting space at, before parting with your marketing budget. Shortlist a few then check them out. Whilst there, talk to stall holders and let them know you are thinking of attending the fair next time around, then ask for their honest feedback. But always go at the end of the day, never at the beginning for 2 reasons:

   1. *You should never interrupt a wedding suppler with your questions at a wedding fair at peak times because you'll be as welcome as a divorce in a marriage! A wedding fair in full flow is the prime opportunity for creatives to promote to potential brides; that is why they are there after all. Come between a supplier and a prospect and you will be seen as a nuisance. Wait for a gap in bridal traffic towards the end of the show when the foot-fall has died down before seeking supplier opinions.*

   2. *Furthermore, by the end of the day, wedding creatives will be able to tell you with much more accuracy if the fair was a success or not.*

- Make it your business to find out who the established wedding creatives are in your industry. Ask them which fairs they attend. The very successful creatives will have an abundance mentality and will willingly share where they go because they realise there are thousands of weddings taking place annually creating more than enough work for everyone.

- Another excellent tip is to target wedding fairs run by borough councils. One of the legal conditions of marriage in the UK is the declaration of wedding banns in the parish in which both persons intending to marry live. This is a rich database of all couple's intent on marrying within their boundaries. These councils are in the perfect position to promote their wedding fair directly to their target audience. It goes without saying that they have a very good chance of pulling in high numbers.

- Established brands running for years will generally produce a more predictable footfall than start ups. If you are new to this form of wedding marketing, begin with the old guard. Medium to big players often run more than 1 fair in different areas with some being more popular than the others. Where choice exists ask your organiser for a recommendation, this will be a good place for you to start.

Wedding fair organisers need fabulous suppliers – wedding suppliers need ready to buy brides. When both needs are met, a cycle of successive fairs is put in motion. So a hallmark for successful wedding fairs is found in the longevity of the event. In fact the very best wedding fair organisers are so good at matching the right suppliers to the right brides, they often sell out or operate at near capacity, have waiting lists of keen suppliers wanting in, and have been running for years.

- During my green years, and before I learnt how to find the best organisers I took a stall from an unknown team launching a new show - 6 brides showed up; my worst experience ever! I've also attended national fairs where thousands of brides came. Both experiences taught me that I want busy fairs with brides arriving all day to avoid boardroom setting in. If you are like me, the minimum number of brides you'll want in attendance to keep your stand fully engaged is 250, any more will be a welcomed bonus.

- Professional organisers will want a well turned out, highly profitable show just as much as you will. Promoters have a plethora of marketing funnels at their disposal to increase the chances of an events success to include: home page website announcements, emails, blogs, word of mouth; plus posts on Facebook, Twitter, LinkedIn, Pintrest, and Instagram. Most show organisers will use all or a mix of the above channels at a minimum. But I've seen some of the biggest show organisers boost awareness to another level by placing ads on some of these paid for platforms:

  - *Internet TV*

  - *Radio*

  - *Newspapers*

  - *Bridal magazines*

  - *Banner adverts*

  - *Billboards*

It goes without saying that the more a show organiser promotes their event the greater the chances of its overall success, so carry out your own due diligence by discovering how your fair will be promoted before deciding to book, the best way to find out is by asking the marketeer selling your stall. That said once you've decided on a wedding show to place your budget, view it as you becoming a part of the wedding fair team. I encourage you to do your marketing bit as well, help promote the fair by announcing your attendance to brides on social media and your website, because you have the power to influence brides into attendance on the day as well. Something as simple as "I will be at the XYZ wedding show on dd/mm/yyyy. Visit me at stand XXX", will be fine.

Looking back on the time I resonated with C:

'I rent spaces at wedding fairs and hope to get one or two bookings to cover the cost of my overheads. Any more is a bonus.'

I do so with a degree of disappointment in the realisation that I set my standards so unacceptably low. I managed my expectations to be happy at breaking even. It demonstrated a lack of drive and ambition to step up and claim my fair share of brides at the fair looking to hire a supplier in my category. I displayed a lack of self-confidence that I did not expect more than one or two couple's to buy from me. I'd conditioned myself for premeditated failure, worst still, I was OK with it. If this resonates with you, and you circled C, then you owe it to yourself to raise your standards and if the wedding creatives around you tell you it's OK to just cover costs at a wedding fair, I'm here to tell you, you are moving in the wrong circles. In fact, without knowing it you are spiralling within an ever decreasing circle, and this is your warning to change that view now if you want to grow your wedding business exponentially. An attitude of being happy breaking even is way too low a benchmark for you. Break free from this limiting thought, elevate your self-worth and adopt a winner's mindset.

If you circled D:

'Wedding fairs are an abundant source of higher paying brides. My goal is to book a considerable proportion of the brides who express an interest in me at a wedding fair, not on the day but as part of my follow-up process.'

The rest of this section will help you get deeper successes.

And if you circled E:

'I have gone full circle, I have an abundance of ideal clients beating a path to my business, I no longer need this strategy.'

Congratulations!

In the first part of this section, I promised to give you a road map to success at wedding fairs, here's the blueprint I recommend for you:

7 Steps to Attract & Book Brides at a Wedding Fair:

1. Apply the 10 minute funnel

Condense your pitch and responses from your prospects to around 10 minutes. Why? Think of your wedding fair as a conveyor belt of potential new business; every minute you spend engaged in conversation with a bride, is a minute saying goodbye to the other brides walking past your stand, because as they walk on by, they do so having been denied the opportunity of learning about how your unique wedding experience can improve their day.

So what should you aim to achieve in around 10 minutes for maximum bookings from your fair?

2. Draw brides in

It starts with a pattern interrupting banner, video or display to compel brides to stop by and want to know more. Your draw is effectively your headline and is the most important attribute of your stand, so carefully plan the mind trigger you'll use to attract brides in.

What attention grabber can you create to demand a bride to think *"Wow! I've got to stop by here"*. Focus solely on the unique benefits you offer and avoid features. The benefits should be compiled of your most desirable USPs and distinguish you from your competitors.

3. Availability

The saying *"Time is money"* is acutely applicable at a wedding fair.

From the moment it opens until closure, a steady stream of potential new business will flow towards you. To maximise on this opportunity one of the first things you'll want to discover is the brides wedding date allowing you to quickly check if you are free. In my early years I would make the schoolboy error of ploughing headlong into my elevator pitch, only to discover at the end of my flow that I was already booked. What a dual waste of time for the bride and I. But there was an even greater waste; I'd missed the one off opportunity to connect and resonate with the other brides passing by, whose date I may have been available on.

4. Passion breeds enthusiasm

Show passion for what you offer, be warm, friendly and smile when you engage in conversation. Brides and grooms buy from experts they know, like and trust and rapport is a powerful motivator in a couples decision making process, so make sure you work it.

5. Generate the expert glow

This is a very important criteria governing the buying choices of discerning couples, so do what you can to ensure your 'Expert Glow' shines. Prospects want the security and peace of mind that comes from consistent and frequent wow factor results. So find ways to establish yourself as a professional, sought-after authority in your niche, as this will ease prospects into wanting to become clients, nudging them further down your funnel.

6. Collect data

If you work the stand alone, set a target to collect around 30 hot leads for follow-up, and up to multiples of 30 for each trained team member attending the fair with you. More on this in the bonus section.

7. Rinse and repeat.

If you get from 1 - 6 successfully, put your couple back on the wedding fair conveyor belt and do it all over again.

Location, location, location

The best organisers carefully plan the walk through of their fair to ensure brides get funnelled to all stands, but if you are quick off the mark you may be able to cherry pick an ideal spot such as the near the entrance, exit or space around the fashion show. So grab one if available at the time of booking, you may pay a premium but it will be worth it.

Is it better to engage in marketing or sales at a wedding fair?

Assuming your fees are higher than average (or will be soon), your target market will be discerning brides and grooms, willing to pay a premium for what you offer as opposed to price shoppers. Your higher paying bride wants something that feels exclusive, professional and reliable. It follows then that you will need to explain your niche in order for prospects to clearly see the added value they will enjoy before booking you, in other words, unless you are already known to the prospect, an impulse buy is unlikely.

For the sake of simplicity, let's assume you are able to deliver your appealing sales pitch in just 30 minutes. Let us also assume your wedding fair runs for 5 hours from 11am to 4pm. We will make a further assumption that your fair attracts 250 brides, and they arrive evenly across the day at a rate of 50 per hour. *("In your dreams Terry, I hear you thinking :)* but humour me and stay with me for a moment...) Under these conditions, the maximum number of 30 minute sales pitches you could possibly deliver is 10 on the day (2 brides per hour x 5 hours). Assuming you work alone at the fair, 48 brides per hour will walk right past you and into the open arms of your competitors because you will not be free to interact with them.

So many brides, so little time

Now let's assume that instead of going to the fair with a proactive intent to sell, your strategy is to gather data to follow-up on a future date. With this approach, instead of restricting yourself to rapport building with just 2 brides per hour, by utilising the 10 minute funnel, you could widen your reach to 6 brides per hour or put another way, a maximum of 30 marketing pitches across the day that you can follow-up on (6 brides per hour x 5 hours). It is for these reasons I recommend short bursts of high impact marketing over 10 minutes (or so), because they will yield a bigger overall return from your fair than by going in with a sales intent to close deals. This is why I conclude, marketing is better than selling at a wedding fair, and is precisely why I personally came away with approximately 30 hot leads to follow up with from at each fair I attended.

With this in mind, imagine what you could achieve with a team at your wedding fair. By training staff to utilise the 10 minute funnel, having two of you on your stand means you could potentially complete the day with 60 leads to follow-up. 3 trained marketeers would help you yield up to 90 leads and so on.

This is not to say you should never take bookings at a fair should a bride want to buy there and then, of course you should. The point is when you take a birds eye view, you could get more bookings long term using the marketing versus an intent to sell strategy because you'll simply be able to reach out to more brides.

Should you collect data at wedding fairs?

Absolutely yes! It can help your business thrive. But how do you get a brides personal contact details? The insider secret is to always arouse interest and excitement in your wedding experience before asking for data. Do a great job with the 10-minute funnel and your ideal bride will be delighted to give you her contact details for follow-up, fail and she will not; brushing you off with "Is it OK if I contact you?" Reading between the lines, this response means you did not connect with your prospects deepest desires, hopes and dreams for her wedding during one or more of the steps of the 10 Minute Funnel.

So if data collection is so beneficial, why do some wedding suppliers avoid it? Lets look at the 3 most popular objections...

Fear of bother

The fear of bother prevents some wedding professionals from fully capitalising on their fairs – as it once did me. The fear of bother is a limiting belief so lets challenge the reasons why some people think they'd present a nuisance to a bride who:

1. *Gave up social time on a Friday, Saturday or Sunday*

2. *Drove to a wedding fair in search of an amazing experience*

3. *Found an ideal wedding supplier*

4. *Listened intently and with interest to the benefits offered*

5. *Liked what they heard*

6. *Enthusiastically gave contact details and permission to follow-up*

In this instance the fear of bother simply does not make sense!

The reason some are reticent to call may actually be rooted on shaky ground; and by sharing a personal experience, I hope to help.

When I started my first business during the late 90's, I clung to a similar limiting belief. It was not until I was in a seminar hosted by a larger than life character who made me challenge and question many things including the origins of my fear of bother was I able to overcome it. The event was called 'Unleash The Power Within' and the mentor who guided me was Tony Robbins.

He helped me trace my fear of bother back to my childhood. As a teenager, I remember my mum cursing under her breath each time a sales person cold called or telephoned our home, trying to sell us something we did not need, nor want. By the time I left home, those negative connotations were well and truly rooted in my brain and I linked sales to bothering people for years. With that negative limiting belief it was no surprise to discover I was rubbish at selling. And guess what? I struggled with follow-up calls and emails as well. I was in such a mess I even began telephone conversations with *"Sorry to bother you…"* What frame of mind do you think I put my bride in with such an awful opening?

Do you think it helped or hindered whatever I said next? But that was the soundtrack of the stuck record that was playing in my mind. Nonetheless, I analysed my beliefs and started to view warm leads through a different paradigm. I accepted they were all from brides who actually wanted what I had to offer. Prospects whom had given up personal information and their explicit permission for me to get in touch! That single revelation flipped my 'fear of bother' to 'they actually need and want my help!' Now when I follow-up, I do so with an inner smile knowing that I can create dream outcomes for brides and grooms and help them get precisely what they desire from their wedding.

By turning my limiting belief into an empowering belief, I can't wait to follow-up. By simply changing the frame of reference I held on callbacks, I created a pillar of success that contributed to massive business growth, and if this resonates with you, you can do the same by simply figuring out what's holding you back from calling or emailing your list.

If you have one, ask *"where does your fear of bother actually come from?"* Go back to the time when it was first introduced into your life. You must have got it from somewhere. Were you in conversation with another wedding supplier who frequently had negative responses to call-backs? Did they voice their bad experiences to you? Did you eventually cloak yourself in someone else's negativity, then believe it?

Some wedding professionals have never been properly trained in tele-marketing and have formed their own patter which may not present them in the best light. The way we communicate on the phone is either constructive or destructive to our businesses. In my own case I was actually 'unselling' prospects with my "Sorry to bother you" opening. Tele-marketing really is easy, in my case it was not because I was making it hard. Once I'd figured out how to think like a bride and communicate like an influential wedding professional, I was off to the races!

To get to the next base with the leads you have worked hard to collect at your wedding fair, learn the art of creating enthusiasm by phone and email. To get you started make sure 90% of what you say offers a benefit driven solution to the problem your bride wants solved and add a touch of curiosity to leave her feeling intrigued to find out more, using the remaining 10% of the time to move your prospect onto the next step, for example a face to face meeting, or whatever the next step in your funnel is.

Spend honest time analysing your beliefs on follow-up. Are they positive or negative? Answering this question is very important because your personal mindset will contribute to whether you are an asset or a liability to the growth of your business. To quote Henry Ford *"Whether you think you can, or you think you can't - you're right."*

I don't need to collect data, if they like me, they'll get in touch and book me

I use to think like this but the reality is, most won't.

Yes it happened a few times but I soon realised the truth that brides may well have liked me at the fair and taken my marketing material home with all the others, but what if my card or brochure got lost and could not be found when the bride was ready to contact me? I'd have no choice but to say goodbye to my lead even if the bride was intent on booking, because what I effectively did was abdicate the responsibility of the booking to the bride when I should have claimed that essential business growing responsibility for myself.

Today I make it super simple for a bride to book me through permission based follow-up that I am in control of and I highly recommend you do the same.

I don't have time to follow-up

I'm 100% with you on this one...

The wedding fair will detonate an administrative time bomb, creating hours of post event follow-up before you will be able to convert your warm leads into clients. Remember it's going to take on average 7 – 12 touches to get booked. But you have to do it because as a wedding creative, most of your sales will come from one-time buyers, so new business will be the bloodline of your wedding business. Without it you will experience cash flow problems.

So invest in an excellent Customer Relationship Management (CRM) system to manage all your interactions with current and future brides. A CRM is capable of sending out personalised, automated time delayed messages on your behalf that look as if they were hand typed by you, using the bride and groom's name, wedding date, venue etc. In fact the templates I use are so effectively wordsmithed, brides often write back responding to my fourth or fifth automated response saying something like "Hi Terry, I am so sorry not to have got back to you sooner, I did receive your previous messages but I had been busy with XY or Z until now, can we meet on ..." They actually think I personally wrote all those messages! The reality is I created the templates years ago, and they continue to sequentially flow out automatically, creating another touch that can potentially lead to a bride buying at some point in the future, whilst I write this book for you, or engage in some other activity. And as long as your emails add value to the bride, are benefit driven and create the certainty of perfection, you will not be seen as spammy, but fail at this hurdle and you will.

I literally have hundreds of leads going on at any one time and I would need a whole admin team to manage them manually, yet my CRM handles them like a breeze. I set it and (almost) forget it. And this is precisely what I advise you do. Go and discover a perfect CRM that automates repetitive tasks in a personalised way that convinces your prospect that you sat at your computer and personally typed it.

OK, having spoken at length on data I want to conclude by giving you a free template to help you ask for the key information you'll need to collect for follow-up.

Bride's Name	
Groom's Name	
Wedding Date	
Wedding Venue	
Mobile Number	
Best Time To Call	
Email Address	

Always use 'slow down boxes' for email capture to prevent prospects scribbling eligibly. The amount of ambiguous email address I got in my early years was so frustrating, there I was sat down and ready to follow-up by email and I had no idea what the scrawl in front of me said. I'm sharing this with you because I don't want you to go through a similar annoyance. If you are tech savvy reduce the possibility of errors even further by getting prospective clients to fill in their data on a tablet or laptop at the fair.

Marketing Pyramid Segment 7:

Paid leads

Buying leads from online wedding directories is a very effective way to get in front of your avatar. If you have calendar gaps and need to accelerate your booking rate of higher paying brides, buy leads.

Back in my early years, when I was uninformed, still dragging buckets, and before the top four segments of my marketing pyramid began to bear low hanging fruit, one of the most successful strategies I stumbled upon was lead purchasing from online wedding directories and I can credit them in going a long way in helping me to survive during my deepest financial struggle. I have a much reduced need for them today because of the effectiveness of my current marketing pyramid but back then I purchased around 70 or so leads a month providing an essential pipeline of prospects. I still dragged buckets though because I had not yet discovered the power of a CRM for the scheduling and auto-responding of emails. I became a slave to admin, and I eventually caved in under the weight of manually managing hundreds of leads which lead to embarrassing errors like emailing or calling prospects inappropriately because I failed to update their status correctly. Learn from my mistake - to make directory lead purchasing work for you, you must get a CRM. The two go hand in glove, it is a poor use of your valuable time to drag buckets in Labour – Zone 2 by managing your database manually.

Remember qualified leads and new business are the lifeblood of your wedding business; without them you will experience cashflow and then personal problems. If your business is in its infancy and you are struggling to get enquiries organically, buy leads in the interim to see you through.

In the past I have personally used UK Bride, The Wedding Guide, Confetti, Wedding Leads, Guides for Brides and Hitched, but there are many other options open to you and this list is by no means extensive or conclusive. Research several wedding directories, test and measure the quality of their data in small amounts until you find a company that works for you. Don't go in big from the start because if the data source does not work for you, you will be locked in for the duration of you contract. Test with the minimum number of leads for the first two months and only if it works should you scale up.

Insider tip: *Always ask the directory salesperson if brides have to check a box saying they are still looking for the service you offer. Some data sellers do not pre-qualify what services the bride still needs and lump all their data together meaning you could potentially receive a ton of leads for brides wanting X whilst you specialist in Y, frustrating both parties.*

What to do with the data you've bought?

Follow-up, follow-up then follow-up again.

Here are some options:

Post

Impress prospects by mailing information or a sample purposefully designed to grab his or her attention, arouses excitement and compel your avatar to take the next step.

Advantages – Nowadays fewer suppliers post opting instead to use the internet, so you'll stand out in a crowded market as prospects physically interact with the quality of your wedding experience.

Disadvantages – Design, creation and shipping costs will eat into profits, and post takes time to be delivered, at least a day unless you use a same day courier which will add considerably to overheads.

Where you are along the business growth curve will be a factor as to whether you opt to post or not. Mature businesses with a healthy cash flow tend to engage in postal communications more than start-ups who need to control costs.

Email

An excellent all-round choice when combined with a CRM capable of sending out your pre-written email campaign automatically.

Advantages – Your message can be delivered in an instant, without the delivery costs associated with the postal method above. You can make frequent touches. The rule is anything you find yourself repeating from prospect to prospect should be automated. As previously mentioned if you buy a database of leads, using a CRM is the most efficient and cost effective way to squeeze the maximum profits out of your monthly data. What's more, your CRM will never 'forget' to send a touch out and it will issue your messages timely, leaving you free to do other things. Some CRM's like MailChimp and Constant Contact even give you useful open rate reports confirming the time, date and frequency as to when your messages was read.

Disadvantages – Eventually your auto responder will get pushed beneath the fold under the weight of incoming messages arriving after yours, and you may become the victim of the saying 'out of sight, out of mind' hence the importance of regular follow-ups.

Your emails may also end up in your prospects spam folder. The bigger CRM's have good deliverability rates because of their reputation and relationships with email clients, but a small percentage will still not get delivered. That said, using a CRM is without doubt the best way to send these types of emails.

It is inevitable that your mail will compete for attention whilst surrounded by the noise of all the other messages flooding into your avatar's inbox, hence the need for expertly wordsmithed copy to gain and maintain interest.

Text

Underestimated and underused.

You are more likely to get a response to a text message than email when your message is sent during working hours because the receiver takes more notice of a text alert than they do an email alert, especially between 9-5. And because text messages tend to be shorter they can be viewed discreetly at work, making them easier to conceal from the bosses watchful eye. Text messages have a much higher deliverability rate and do not end up in spam folders. And because fewer marketeers use text to communicate to brides, your message will have much less marketing noise around it, you will have more of your couple's attention and your text will stay visible longer, and not get pushed beneath the fold anywhere nearly as quickly as it will in an email account.

The downside is your message is unlikely to be long and detailed so it can be difficult to convey all you wish to say. Used strategically though, text messages are a super way to grab a couple's attention and move them onto the next step towards booking you.

Marketing Pyramid Segment 8:

Paid Facebook Advertising

Facebook adverts appear alongside posts from families and friends based on demographics, but what's most important to you is that Facebook is where your brides are hanging out right now and it is no wonder wedding business owners are advertising on Facebook more and more to reach their potential customers with well-targeted adverts and copy that resonates with their niche market. For example you can select to target: Females showing an engaged status, between the ages of 24 and 45 who live in a 50 mile radius of you. You can set daily limits that turn your advert off once your budget has depleted putting you in complete control of your spend. Use your advert to drive your target audience to a landing page on your website giving more information about your offer then guide them down to the next step in your sales funnel.

In other words, through carefully wordsmithed copy, you can position yourself directly in the crosshairs of your avatar on Facebook immediately. The insider secret is in knowing how to craft your advert in such a powerfully compelling way that you alter the course of what your prospect intended to do - socialise, and pattern interrupt her to do what you want her to do - wedding planning, with your services front of mind.

Facebook Advertising works. Some say it does not, what does not work are poorly written adverts that fail to engage with their target audience. If you have tried advertising on Facebook and failed it was your advert, not Facebook. If you struggle, simply send an email to: thrive@weddingmarketingmastery.co.uk and I'll point you in the right direction to getting better results.

Marketing Pyramid Segment 9:

Free Facebook Posts, Twitter and LinkedIn

These social networking sites are excellent ways to show off the multi-facets of your personality and great for reminding people what you do. I recommend keeping your Facebook Personal Page mainly for your social life, but make sure you remind friends and family what you do infrequently so they are aware of the wedding services you offer, allowing you to benefit from the odd word of mouth referral.

For regular posting about your company successes and activities, use your Facebook Business Page. Each time you work at a wedding, post pictures and comments of your work. If you have an exciting news release, or had a professional success, let your connections know about it. And whenever you receive glowing testimonials add it to your Page so your tribe knows what past clients think about you. This builds confidence in your brand and provides independent social proof which trumps anything you may say about how wonderful you are.

LinkedIn is mainly B2B. It is a powerful way to let other wedding creatives know what you do and is a definite source of new business, or a way to rekindle old business contacts if used creatively. Let me give you 2 examples: Remember the story where Maria moved on from Dartmouth House resulting in work for myself grinding to a halt? My friend Tony Winyard was also recommended at that venue and mentioned he had also noticed enquiries had dried up and came up with a creative idea using LinkedIn to track her down using her LinkedIn profile. Tony discovered she had joined a new prestigious venue and said he was going to call her and suggested I did the same. I rang, and after a catch-up she introduced me to the wedding co-ordinator and with Maria's endorsement I was listed at the new venue as a preferred supplier. All because of the power of LinkedIn. In another instance I was contacted by a wedding co-ordinator at a beautiful 5 star venue near Covent Garden who discovered my LinkedIn profile. I was invited in for a meeting and after a successful chat / interview I was then asked to become a preferred supplier. Without LinkedIn it is unlikely that I would have got the listing.

Social networking is an effective way to gain new business and even though I personally place it at the base of my own marketing pyramid do not under estimate the new business to be gained by being a part of the social networking family. The potential revenues are huge.

Summary

There are a plethora of ways to market your wedding business outside of the strategies I've suggested, but unless you have a large marketing department and a large budget, I recommend learning to master just a few that you can stay on top of. By way of summary, let me explain why I recommend you prioritise your pyramid (at least the top 4) in the identical order to which I've stacked my own.

Lay pipelines with Golden and Other Word of Mouth Opportunities

I believe in, and practice the principle of working hard today in order to make tomorrows work easier. And this is accomplished through:

1. *'The Golden Triangle'*
   Becoming a preferred supplier at luxury venue's, and

2. *The other word of mouth pipelines*
   From wedding professionals and guests who refer business to you.

Of the 9 strategies I recommend, your 'Golden Triangle and other word of mouth pipelines' will require the hardest amount of work, take the longest amount of time to harvest but when you eventually reap the rewards, these sources will deliver a lucrative income stream of low hanging fruit for the lifetime of your relationships with your venues and the people you network with. By focusing on your 'Golden Triangle and other word of mouth pipelines' you can do the hard work once, then get valuable referrals for many years after. Laying these pipelines is passive marketing at its best. In this zone you work smart not hard. I have networking relationships with a number of the best suppliers in the wedding industry. I am busy and no longer worry about where my next job will come from because of my Golden Triangle and other word of mouth pipelines. There is nothing stopping you from doing the same, other than taking action.

'Dragging buckets with one hit wonders'

The other strategies work but serve up one hit wonders, meaning you will have to drag buckets by hustling them continuously, and in most cases at a cost. My advice is to use the one hit wonder strategies whilst building your business or during quite times but your primary long-term marketing objective should be to structure a powerful Golden Triangle and other word of mouth pipelines capable of sustaining you.

Final food for thought

Wedding entrepreneurs who focus on the bottom of the marketing pyramid will always work harder for business than those who choose to capitalise on the riches at the top of the marketing pyramid. Which will you focus on?

THE ELEVENTH HABIT

Don't Allow Your Inbox to Boss You Around

Before I got into effective work habits, I was addicted to distractions. I'd wake, check Facebook and emails then allow the notifications and messages to boss me around, reacting to whatever distraction the incoming email or post requested of me. I had no priorities for the day and was blown around like a leaf in the autumn wind by message after message. Can you relate to this? Thinking back if I worked that way during my corporate days, I'd have been fired! Do you need to fire yourself and re-hire a new you?

Tony Robbins and Brendon Burchard are both mentors to whom I will be forever thankful to because of the wisdom they taught me including their guidance on not going through a 'to do list' daily for the sake of being busy, instead they got me focused on the outcomes I needed to achieve daily, weekly and monthly to mark progress on my business. They got me to carry out whatever activities were necessary to get the desired results with the minimum of distractions. With their help I got comfortable putting my phone on the 'do not disturb' setting during my 'Money Hours' so I could maximise productivity. I got more done by blocking periods of time out to focus on a single task instead of multitasking, and by focusing on one single project or task at a time I began to get measurable results that moved the needle of my wedding business forward. I owned up to the fact that the regular non urgent interruptions created by email and social media alerts prevented me from completing my daily priorities and actually diverted me to working on the priorities of other people. I learnt to come back to emails, voicemails and other notifications during my 'off-peak zones' once I had done what I needed to do to take care of my own house, and this was one of the biggest disciplines I practised that sent my business north, and it has the power to do the same for you; you just need to be open to giving it a try. Most people will happily wait a few hours for a response to a request, and still thank you for your quick reply, but more importantly you'll get more done.

You owe it to yourself, your business and to the people who depend on you for their standard of living to stop the impulsive knee-jerk reactions to the 'instructions' of others the minute they ping into your computer or phone. Let me put it another way, imagine you are driving your car and plan a route from A to B. Now imagine every few moments a person you are driving past randomly shouts out *"At the next junction turn left"*, or *"Turn right"* or *"Make a U turn"*, and you do, driving further and further off course from your intended destination. It goes without saying that you'll lengthen the time it will take you to get to point B following other people's random instructions, if you get there at all! Well each time you allow an alert to interrupt your workflow this is precisely what you are doing. Yes sometimes an urgent message pings in demanding a response but I'm not talking about those. You'll find it's your impulsive knee-jerk reaction that drives your workflow and thought processes off course by working on other people's priorities the moment they land in your inbox. This is one of the fastest ways to dilute your productivity and allow others to derail you, effectively sucking the oxygen out of your business. If you rarely fulfil the priorities you set yourself at the start of each day, you may find the answer in the realisation that your boss is really your inbox, because IT and not you, directed your day.

If this speaks directly to you, let me ask you something: *"If you don't drive your business forward intelligently from A to B, who will?"*

If this poignant question presents a moment of truth for you, as it once did for me, promise yourself you will change in this instant, because the success of your wedding business depends on, and is inextricably linked to the sum total of your daily achievements.

THE TWELFTH HABIT

Winners Think Differently, It's Time To Reset Your Mindset

Each day you live you are given another 86,400 seconds.

Think of a wedding professional in your industry whose success you would like to emulate. Get them really clear and focused in your mind. Now here's the thing, that wedding professional is gifted with the same 86,400 seconds as you! The reason you are getting different results is because of the different ways in which you both use your 86,400 seconds. The good news is by adopting the 12 Habits into the fabric of your business, you will put yourself on the fastest path to sustainable success and close the gap.

I know what follows does not apply to you, but I have met, listened to and been dismayed by wedding professionals who point the finger at everyone else for their lack of success. They blame the universe for their current conditions and lazily hope the universe will one day change course around them charting an easy route for their success. They complain "It's alright for so and so, they've got X, Y and Z"... and on and on they go giving excuse after excuse as to why they cannot advance. They effectively tie the favourable circumstances of the successful to their own misfortunes and as long as they hold that false link in their minds they make it impossible to break free and improve their own circumstances. They are paralysed by their own thoughts into thinking it will never happen for them. In reading The 12 Habits, I don't believe this to be a fallacy you hold, because you and I both know that it's nothing to do with a person's advantages of connections, education, the government, economy, money, family or any of the other excuses 'victims' give for not being where they want to be, because for every person who had a privileged head-start in life and business, there is another person who made it against the odds. It is not our past nor outside influences that we have no control over that determine whether we succeed or fail; it's the influences inside our heads, our core beliefs about our worth and who we believe we can become, and the type of action we take on a daily basis with the 86,400 seconds we are given that paves our destiny. Our future is in our hands, our future is molded by the precious way we use the daily seconds we are gifted with by God. Our future is down to us... our future is down to you and me.

Step up and aim for the top. You have it within you to become the niche expert that brides and venue's pursue whenever they think about your profession. Never settle on just being another player in your industry, you want to be the winner. Raise your bar way above the mediocrity of being beige. Reject doing the identical things the masses do in your field of expertise. The cream are different. The cream always rise to the top, and the cream always get booked first. Believe in yourself, as I believe in you, because in reading thus far, I know you want your time to be now. And whenever you begin to doubt you are ready, take inspiration from this quote from Hillel the Elder:

"If not now, when? If not you, who?"

Winners have to win, constantly and consistently. At the time of writing Usain Bolt is the fastest man on earth but he is not content with his time, he wants to smash his own world record. His goal is to dominate, to win. It matters not that the example is of a sports star. Winners in every field, including your own are driven by a similar mindset. Winners although gracious in defeat, hate losing, they don't compete on the same playing field as the masses. They compete in their minds, against themselves. For a true winner, winning is everything. On another level, true winners are also very generous and give back by using their expertise and experience to help elevate others because winners like seeing people they care about succeed.

Mind

First and foremost you must develop an unshakable self-belief in your ability to succeed. Expand your mind daily by learning from entrepreneurs who have achieved what you are seeking to achieve, remember my friend Abbey's first lesson? In so doing you will short cut your learning curve and arrive at your income, lifestyle and freedom goals quicker. The fastest path to becoming a master is through following the path of a master, someone who has walked the walk before you and demonstrated success in the areas you want to succeed. The greatest people in the world have mentors, coaches, advisors and are in mastermind groups and you need to do the same. Heightened and sustained success at any level is never achieved through solidarity, but through the distilled wisdom cascaded down from a mentor or panel of experts. Do it the experts way first, after mastering theirs, do it your way.

Crave lifelong learning and mastery, achieve it and that which you desire will eventually be yours.

Focus

Become completion orientated. How many projects capable of transforming your life have you given up way too early because it got a little tough, or your eyes flitted onto the next shiny new thing?

Focus on creating your positive advantage. You know what additional skills and attractions you'll need to get under your belt to orchestrate your own success. You know that having no USPs means no positive advantage. No positive advantage means no fast track to success. No fast track to success means fighting it out with the masses leading to a cycle of famine and feast and I'd never want that for you, so promise yourself to focus on hauling a plethora of USPs. Begin with this end in mind it's a proven route to being able thrive not survive.

Start the big projects you believe will lead you to success, and more importantly, complete what you start. Remember procrastination is no longer for you. If you do want help with procrastination, read *Eat That Frog!* by Brian Tracy.

Having read this far you now have the formula to elevate your income and lifestyle level by becoming a client magnet to high paying brides and grooms. But the ingredients to this formula won't mix themselves. You'll have to mix them daily, using The 12 Habits as your guide.

From here on out you will either make a choice to self-develop or shelf-develop. You can take this book and place it on your shelf for no further development at all letting it gather dust, or you can use The 12 Habits to continue your journey of self-development and accelerate your path to success in order to live your life at the highest level and take care of those you love and care for.

Either way you are saying "Yes" to something; either you are saying "Yes" to procrastination, stagnation and continued average pay and bookings or "Yes" to kick-starting your business, getting paid exponentially and becoming the higher paying client magnet you know you can be.

What are you going to say "Yes" to?

REACH UP TO THE NEXT LEVEL

Thank you for reading The 12 Habits. It's an indicator that you want better for yourself and for those who depend on you for their standard of living. From now on, make a promise to take action on what you have learnt daily and hold onto your vision of success, no matter what.

My hope is that The 12 Habits provided all the impetus you need to grow your business by shortening your learning curve and illuminating your fastest route to success. If this is the case, it was an honour serving you.

But if you feel a little overwhelmed and need my help implementing The 12 Habits you are not alone, come and join the growing number of students taking their businesses to the next level using my one-to-one or online courses.

To continue our relationship:

Visit: www.weddingmarketingmastery.co.uk

Or email: thrive@weddingmarketingmastery.co.uk

Finally, please take a moment to comment on The 12 Habits, search for: 12 Habits Of Successfully Booked Up Wedding Suppliers on Amazon.com in the books section and leave your review there.

TESTIMONIALS

"A massive thanks to Terry Lewis and his mentoring programme. I had been stuck charging around £200 for over 15 years when I bumped into a friend at a networking event. He recommended Terry's 1-1 mentoring programme and after 6 months on his programme I converted my first five out of five enquiries into bookings for weddings with an average fee of £1,475! I definitely had to up my game and stretch myself, but I now know its possible.

Thanks again Terry for all your insights and encouragement. It has been so worth it."

Chris Anthony

"Dear Terry. Thank you for completely turning my business around! I've started to see measurable results after implementing the strategies and ideas that you suggested, and I am now currently achieving massive improvements in my conversion rates from leads into bookings!

My business is taking off at an amazing rate as a direct result of your guidance and mentoring and with your continued support you are keeping me on track in smashing my goals and ambitions, and then setting even higher ones!

I couldn't recommend you highly enough. Can't wait until our next session!"

Zoe Alexandria

"...We implemented a number of the suggestions and techniques ...and twelve months later have increased the average booking fee beyond the level we expected. For anyone looking to understand the requirements of attracting high end brides and wanting some proven techniques I couldn't recommend a better starting place."

Steve Bradshaw

"Just a few short years ago I would not have believed where I would get to with my wedding business.

Terry's help, advice and guidance has been invaluable to me and has helped me focus on where to find my clients and how to ensure they book with me too.

Thank You Terry"

Neil Johnson

"Hi Terry, Wow! What a morning...I really wasn't expecting such a gift...all those pointers and inspirational ideas. Thank you for your time and for sharing. Perhaps you could let me know more about your mentoring and how it works?"

Sarah Martin

"Thanks for organising such an informative and enlightening day. I think far too much emphasis has been put on performance training and not enough on the business side – especially with regards high-value brides/venue.

I thought the content was excellent and your style of presenting made for a very enjoyable day. Not once did I look at watch to see what time it was, which is a good sign!

It's always great being in a room of similar and 'higher-level' peers – keeps the inspiration & drive to be better at full speed."

Iain Baker

"Hi Terry. I would like to start by thanking you for taking the time in putting on the seminar yesterday and sharing some key information I am a bit overwhelmed by the amount of information that I have and am slowly starting to act on things to improve myself.

I have started my new journey already by increasing my fees. I really appreciate the time you took yesterday with the seminar and feel I have learned so much and gained some valuable contacts within the industry."

Phill Makepeace

KEYNOTES, WORKSHOPS & EDUCATION

If you need a keynote workshop or day of wedding education for your organisation, packed with actionable content, I'd be delighted to help.

Call +44 (0) 7974 123 567

Email: thrive@weddingmarketingmastery.co.uk

Online: www.weddingmarketingmastery.co.uk

ACKNOWLEDGEMENTS

Harry Kilb, thank you for the beautiful design. You have given the book an extra dimension and I really appreciate the work you have put into it.

For all your design requirements Harry can be contacted in the following ways: **harry@kilb.co.uk   +44 (7941) 880 370**

Ross Harvey, thank you for your advice, help and guidance over the years, my progress would have been slowed without you.

Ross is one of the worlds finest destination wedding photographers and all images in this book are credited to him, except for the back cover.

How to contact Ross: **www.rossharvey.com   +44 (7764) 740 824**

Tony Winyard, **Gary Evans**, **Barney Grossman**, **Brian Mole** and **Paul Taylor**, I can't thank you enough for your friendship and advice in critiquing this book ahead of publication.

Tony, Gary, Barney, Brian and Paul are all exceptional Master of Ceremonies and DJ's.

How to contact Tony: **www.awe-dj.co.uk**
                          +44 (0) 7771 894 560

How to contact Gary: **www.garyevansweddings.co.uk**
                          +44 (0) 7722 282 037

How to contact Barney: **www.partyeventsunlimited.co.uk**
                          +44 (0) 7840 444 522

How to contact Brian: **www.dancemix.co.uk**
                          + 44 (0) 7941 191194

How to contact Paul: **www.thepartydj.co.uk**
                          +44 (0) 7973 617 153

Paul Young, **Hollie Kamel** and **Kardy Laguda**, thank you for your friendship and years of support which you've extended into proofing the manuscript, I really appreciate the time you took to go over it and value your feedback.

Paul Young is a business advisor and can be reached on:
+44 (0) 7930 314 242

Hollie is a professional singer and you may contact her in the following ways: **www.hollieyourweddingsinger.co.uk**
+44 (0) 7533 509 420

Kardy Laguda is an author and fitness guru and can be reached in the following ways: **www.sevenessentials.net**
www.kardysfitness.com
+44 (0) 7860 468 222

Wedding industry experts:

Damian Bailey, Founder and Managing Director at The Wedding Industry Awards. Damian Bailey is also an award winning wedding photographer with over 500 weddings under his belt.

Alison Hargreaves is Director at Guides for Brides providing wedding directory services to brides and groom's and professional help and advice to wedding professionals. Alison also founded the 5* Customer Service Wedding Awards.

Thank you both for your industry reviews, I sincerely appreciate the forewords you have given.

How to contact Damian:
www.the-wedding-industry-awards.co.uk
www.damianbailey.com

How to contact Alison: **www.guidesforbrides.co.uk**

Fola Ademoye, thank you for working on this manuscript and over 30 years of friendship. You are a wonderfully gifted person and I am very lucky to be in your inner circle.

Fola is an English and French teacher as well as a writer and professional proof reader.

How to contact Fola: **+44 (0) 7956 417 381**

And finally to my partner **Julie Morrow**, thank you for your support, belief and encouragement to help me get this, my first book done. But more importantly, thank you for picking up the scattered pieces of my life and handing them back to me...in the right order. I love you and will never forget all that you have done and continue to do for me.